CHRISTIE'S
TOY RAILWAYS

CHRISTIE'S
TOY RAILWAYS

HUGO MARSH

WITH CONTRIBUTIONS BY PIERCE CARLSON

PAVILION

This edition first published in Great Britain in 2002 by
PAVILION BOOKS LIMITED
64 Brewery Road, London, N7 9NT
www.chrysalisbooks.co.uk
A member of **Chrysalis** Books plc

DESIGNED BY: Balley Design Associates

A CIP catalogue record for this book is available
from the British Library

ISBN 1 86205 525 4

Set in Perpetua
Colour origination by Classic Scan Pte Ltd, Singapore
Printed in Italy by Giunti Industrie Grafiche
1 2 3 4 5 6 7 8 9 10

This book can be ordered direct from the publisher.
Please contact the Marketing Department.
But try your bookshop first.

ABOUT CHRISTIE'S

The name of Christie's is identified throughout the world with art, expertise and connoisseurship.

In 1766 James Christie opened his London auction house and launched the world's first fine art auctioneers. Christie's reputation was established in its early years, when James Christie's saleroom became a fashionable gathering place for Georgian society, as well as for knowledgeable collectors and dealers. Christie offered artists the use of his auction house to exhibit their works and enjoyed the friendship of many of the leading figures of the day such as Sir Joshua Reynolds, Thomas Chippendale and Thomas Gainsborough. Christie's saleroom conducted the greatest auctions of the eighteenth and nineteenth centuries, selling works of art that now hang in the world's most prestigious museums.

Over its long history, Christie's has grown into the world's leading auction house, offering sales in over eighty separate categories, which include all areas of the fine and decorative arts, collectibles, wine, sporting memorabilia, motor cars, even sunken cargo. There are hundreds of auctions throughout the year, selling objects of every description and catering to collectors at every level.

Buyers and browsers alike will find that Christie's galleries offer changing exhibitions to rival any museum. Unlike most museums, however, in the salerooms you can touch each object and examine it up close.

Auctions are an exciting way to buy rare and wonderful objects from around the world. In the salerooms is a treasure trove of items and, while some works may sell for prices that cause a media frenzy, many of the items offered at Christie's are affordable to even the novice collector.

Christie's has had a long involvement with toy railways. It started selling them with model trains in 1966, continuing through the heady and inflationary days of the 1970s and early 1980s with popular sales at the Brighton Engineerium. The Christmas Trains Galore sales at South Kensington started in 1986 and have proved to be very successful ever since; they are also a popular social event for collectors from around the world. Since the late 1980s, Christie's has held numerous landmark auctions, selling several record-breaking collections of Märklin trains, the Bianco Hornby-Dublo Collection and The Tony Matthewman Trix Collection, as well as many extremely fine family collections of Hornby and Bassett-Lowke 0 Gauge trains.

The world of toy trains is vast. The dominant names – Märklin, Hornby and Lionel, with Bassett-Lowke, Bing and Carette following behind – have produced toy trains at various times from 1859, almost as long as there have been railway networks. Remarkably, some rare and beautiful trains produced in Germany during the Golden Age between 1900 and 1914 still survive, although the finest will probably not be seen on the open market for many years. When they do appear, they are extremely expensive.

below: *This Märklin Gauge I "Draisine"*

track inspection car dates from around 1902.

INTROD

Therefore, for many collectors, the greatest focus of interest is the interwar period: of the good-quality material that can still be found, a large proportion of the locomotives, carriages and accessories were made between 1918 and 1940. Hornby and Bing had similar production philosophies, offering the buying public large ranges of quality toy railways at middle-market prices. They sold in enormous quantities and are the mainstay of auctions and swapmeets today. Until 1939 Bassett-Lowke and Märklin, on the other hand, offered more varied ranges of fine quality toys, selling relatively few of the more expensive pieces. Consequently, there are wonderful pieces that hardly, if ever, appear for sale – you can get a taste of such wish-list locomotives, coaches and sets here, but original catalogues show the much broader range on offer in the heyday of toy railways. Fortunately, many catalogues have been reprinted in recent years.

Although much more interwar stock survives than pre-1914 models, several factors have contributed to the scarcity of many pieces. As playthings, trains tended to appeal to older boys who

UCTION

had the patience and skill to operate them, but however careful they were, some damage was likely to result if the pieces were in constant use on a layout. Numbers were further reduced as many train sets fell victim to maternal guilt in the post-war years of shortages. This dictated that when a teenager reached a certain age he should give up such simple pursuits and see his precious set shunted off to a needy cousin or the local Scout group. Such well-meaning gestures created a deprived generation that has since tried to buy back its childhood. It is certainly noticeable with collectors that the seed of interest is first sown early on, even if there is a long hiatus before it germinates.

above: *This 0 Gauge Santa Fe General Motors F3 diesel locomotive was one of the finest models made by Lionel after World War II.*

It is surely difficult for a child today to comprehend that new toys were not openly available in Europe in the late 1940s. Anyone lucky enough to receive a train set would have had it on order months before. One owner selling a Hornby-Dublo set at Christie's recounted how he considered himself very fortunate to have received it for Christmas 1948, and attributed his good luck to the fact that his uncle

worked for Meccano. In the days before electronic games, boys would stay gripped by the toy railway bug

until fourteen or fifteen – and many remain so today.

below: *The design for this German painted lead train, c. 1870, was never updated from the look of the 1840s.*

After years of post-war restrictions, the 1960s brought a new market boom, and a new

style of manufacture. Over the years Hornby Railways has rethought its whole range, and

today's Bachmann and Hornby Railways from China are like fine-scale models, with incred-

ible detailing. By comparison, earlier Hornby-Dublo locomotives seem unrealistically toy-

like, although when first made, it was the finest integrated 00 Gauge railway for children ever produced.

Toy train collecting today is reaching stages of unimagined perfection. Just before and after World War

II, Swiss connoisseurs began seeking early pieces from around 1900, with US collectors joining in to pursue

early American makes during the 1950s. By the 1960s, the hobby had become far more widespread. Instead

of collecting "prodigy" pieces for display, collectors would run and enjoy old Hornby or Lionel pieces.

Wealthy, serious collectors now have most of the pieces they seek, but when a long-sought item

comes on the market, they will pay an extraordinarily high price for it. At the opposite end, the

market has been relatively static for common

or moderately rare pieces in fair condition. Many collectors, though, are happy to run their locomotives and

stock, not minding at all that their value is less than for pieces in mint condition. The pleasure enjoyed more

than offsets the hypothetical financial gain. For a new collector, auctions are generally the best place to begin.

Christie's catalogues contain as much relevant detail as possible, giving objective notes on

condition, while auction estimates are a good price guide.

To cover in detail the complete history of toy trains would take several books this size,

so this is but a brief excursion into their fascinating history, with illustrations from the

archives of Christie's and several leading collectors. I hope it will give the uninitiated a taste of the enjoyment

of toy trains, and also prove enlightening to the more experienced collector. Handling thousands of pieces at

auctions over many years has given me great pleasure, but it has been an equal pleasure to meet knowledge-

able and dedicated collectors around the world, for whom Binns Road, Göppingen or Irvington – the homes

of Hornby, Märklin and Lionel respectively – were paradise on earth.

above: These traditional painted wooden toys date from around 1910 and come from the Erzegebirge region of Saxony, Germany.

chapter 1

THE EARLY HISTORY OF RAILWAYS

Manufacturers sprang up to supply the expanding market and every country had different ideas about what toy trains should look like.

GREAT BRITAIN

Britain was the birthplace of the railway. By the time George Stephenson was experimenting with steam locomotion at the beginning of the nineteenth century, stationary steam engines had been in use for over 100 years and most commercial operators used them for pumping or for rope-hauling rakes of wagons. Creating a mobile power source, however, was a radical move. By 1814, at the age of only 33, Stephenson had built his first locomotive, "Blücher", for the Killingworth Colliery; and in 1823 he opened his locomotive works with his son Robert. On 27 September 1825 the Stockton and Darlington Railway opened, for which the Stephensons created "Active" (better known by her subsequent name "Locomotion"), which became the first steam locomotive to haul passengers on a public railway – albeit at 24kmh (15mph).

The heyday of the Railway Age is seen as a Victorian phenomenon, but the construction of the world's first railway between two cities – Liverpool and Manchester – was very much of the Georgian era. With construction work entrusted to George Stephenson, on 20 April 1829 the proposers of the railway foreshadowed another Victorian convention by organizing a competition for motive power on the new line. Rope haulage was still under consideration and one of the five entrants was horse-drawn, but the three serious contenders were George and Robert Stephenson's "Rocket", Timothy Hackworth's "Sans Pareil" and John Braithwaite's "Novelty". Trials began at Rainhill on 6 October that year.

Down at the station, a waiting crowd is looking for the train, the major event in the town's day. In the distance there is a faint plume of smoke and the sound of a whistle. A tiny shape grows larger and larger and then, with a rush, all flying cinders, heat and bell ringing, the train comes hissing, blowing and clanking up the rails, to come to a gliding stop in front of the apprehensive but excited passengers. Children get their first close look at the prime mover of the Industrial Age, the steam engine.

above: *A Stevens Model Dockyard "dribbler" locomotive with radially set axles, c. 1870, intended to run on floors. They remained in production into the 1930s.*

And then, with a whistle shriek, it is gone in a cloud of smoke and steam. These fearsome machines, under the total control of the brave and steely-eyed engineer, were willing to take you to the ends of the Earth. What child wouldn't want one of their own, scaled down, to play with like a pet? Toy trains must have been widely available from the very beginning of the Railway Age, but few of the earliest ones have survived – toys were made to be played with, broken and then thrown away so that new ones could be bought.

Special grandstands were erected to accommodate the crowds of up to 15,000 who came to view these modern miracles over the following days. The stipulations in the rules concerning weight, power and durability were very specific and demanding. Each locomotive was allowed a run-in and run-out distance, but had to cover a 2.4km (1¹/2 mile) course at top speed both ways to emulate the length of the completed railway. The "Rocket" not only achieved this, but surpassed expectations, winning the handsome prize of £500. She went on to haul trains at the grand opening of the Liverpool and Manchester Railway on 15 September 1830, meeting up with the unfortunate William Huskisson, who became the first railway fatality.

The "Rocket" looks quaint to modern eyes. She weighed only 4.7 tons, but was capable of hauling a full load at 46kmh (29mph). She is preserved today in the Science Museum in London and has recently undergone detailed examination to determine the many changes made to her over the years. Even at the Rainhill Trials she was still under development; her cylinders were lowered to an 8-degree slant soon after and her wooden wheels replaced with stronger cast iron ones. By modern standards, she was basic – she was not even fitted with brakes – but two principles in her construction remained in use for all subsequent steam locomotives. Stephenson himself realized that natural convection alone was not enough to bring up or maintain the heat output of a locomotive firebox; he therefore redirected exhaust steam up the chimney, creating a strong draft through the boiler. This was then combined with Henry Booth's invention of the multi-tube boiler. The use of twenty-five tubes rather than one or two greatly increased the speed of movement and the surface area of interaction between the hot air from the firebox and the water in the boiler. The formula was unbeatable then and remains so today.

As the nineteenth century progressed, iron roads criss-crossed the industrialized nations, but no other country could compare with Britain for the density of its rail system. All England was connected by tracks owned by the giant railway companies, and every company had its own distinctive livery. London and Southwestern had apple green locomotives and coaches painted salmon pink and brown; Midland trains were deep crimson red "lake" with elaborate lining; and the Great Western and the Great Northern locos ran in different shades of green, with coaches of chocolate and cream (Great Western) or natural varnished teak (Great Northern). Caledonian painted its locos a brave blue and the Premier Line was almost alone in having black engines heading white and deep plum brown coaches. "Improved engine green" was what the London Brighton and South Coast called the yellow ochre paint, the colour of autumn leaves, that distinguished their diminutive engines.

below: A rare example of a pre-1900 British train. The cab is completely open and there are no ends to the simple coach.

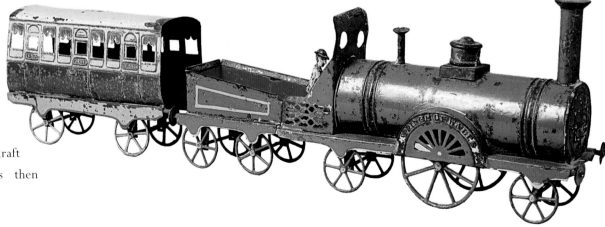

Undersized, uncluttered and brightly varnished, British trains looked like toys. Perhaps that is an explanation for the mystery of why there are so few early toy trains found in England. For the country that invented the railway and was the home of the greatest concentration of railway enthusiasts, this is an enigma. A small number of specialist manufacturers – Newton, Bateman (which had been founded as early as 1774), H.J. Wood, John Theobald, Lucas and Davis among them – made steam-powered toy locomotives from brass, typically with four or six wheels and usually without a tender. These were usually floor runners, although strip track was available, and were nicknamed "dribblers" for their messy running habits. Stevens Model Dockyard (founded 1843) and Clyde Model Dockyard (1789) were both manufacturers and retailers. Heavy and relatively expensive, these toys were only sold through a few

below: An early English brass "dribbler" that ensured plenty of soggy floors. It could have been made any time before World War I.

outlets. The more expensive engines were finished in natural brass with oxidized brass decoration and lining; the cheaper ones had tinplate parts painted dark green with brass wheels and fittings. A few pieces of rolling stock in polished mahogany were offered, but no accessories because these were serious, scientific toys. The locomotive designs were almost all cabless antiques from the dawn of the railway age, unchanged for decades. Stevens Model Dockyard was still cataloguing these fossils well into the 1920s.

There were not many other toy train makers. Wallworks made a small line of cast iron trains, following what appear to be Great Western broad-gauge prototypes. There were a couple of locomotives and some six-wheel coaches. William Britain produced a small mechanical train made of lead, which was propelled around a circle by a rod that extended from a separate clock motor located in the centre. Other than one painted train (see page 15) and some lithographed two-dimensional trains which occasionally turn up, this limited selection seems to have been all that was manufactured in the country that was the leading industrial power of the nineteenth century and the home of the railway.

USA

In the United States, the situation and the market were very different. The population was thinly spread and labour was in chronically short supply, especially skilled labour. To be successful, a firm had to have a factory that could provide large numbers of inexpensive toys, simply made, and then distribute them around a vast country. The output of these factories was huge, and some toys were made in the hundreds of thousands. The earliest toy trains were made from sheet tin formed into a few simple

shapes and soldered together, crudely painted and decorated in stencils of floral designs used widely on the tin household items of the time. Whimsical and charmingly toy-like, these early toys all had to have a large cab, a bell, a lamp, a tall smokestack and, finally, a cowcatcher. This prow-shaped device, painted red and fastened to the front of the engine, was designed to throw to one side any trespassing bovine as the train thundered along to its next destination. No American child wanted a toy train that was not equipped with a cowcatcher.

Once these design criteria had been met, the manufacturers were not particularly concerned with any further attempts at realism, and the designs continued, unchanged, for decades. In the 1890s Ives was still cataloguing tin trains that looked identical to those marketed fifty years before. Novelties were popular and Ives had several, such as the automatic "Whistler" and the "Smoker", which produced clouds of very realistic smoke from a cigarette pushed down the chimney and puffed by a cylinder connected to the wheels. A children's nursery full of tobacco smoke was of not much concern to anyone in those days.

Some of the toys had clockwork mechanisms, and in 1856 the George Brown Co. manufactured one of the

first, a small locomotive with three wheels. It had two large driving wheels up front and a small swivelling one at the rear that could be adjusted so that the train could run around in various-sized circles. Ives had a particularly sinister clockwork design called the "Rocket". When the mechanism ran down, a cap made a bang and a powerful spring caused the locomotive to scatter its parts in all directions, simulating a boiler explosion.

Clockwork was relatively expensive, so the vast majority were simple floor runners, moving under hand power alone. The locomotives were given wonderful names such as "Vulcan", "Orion", "Venus", "Pegasus", "Giant", "Grand Duke", and

top: A Beggs live-steam locomotive and coach dating from around 1880–1900.

above: An American IXL locomotive made by Fallows. This type of tin floor-running toy was made for about fifty years with virtually no changes.

"Adonis". Tracks were never provided for these early toys, and if a station was needed, a shoe box would do. Of the major early manufacturers – Francis, Field and Francis, Schlesinger, Althof Bergman, Stevens and Brown, George Brown, Fallows (IXL) and Ives – only Ives was still in business by 1900.

Wooden trains were appealing to manufacturers because the trains could be built up from basic blocks,

below: Cast iron is the archetypal nineteenth-century American toy material, here used to good effect to produce a sturdy but attractive bogie car.

circles, rods and turnings, but they really came into their own in the early 1870s with the development of colour lithography. A few earlier trains made use of black printing on coloured paper and there were even some toys that used hand tinting, but the advent of multi-coloured lithographs meant that imaginatively detailed and brightly coloured paper sheets could simply be glued on to a plain wooden train to bring it to life. The locomotive driver was usually shown as a debonair figure. The hard-working stoker was included, and a typical range of passengers variously smoked cigars, read the papers, looked out of the windows and generally seemed to be having a good time.

Wooden trains had more realistic proportions than the tin ones and a few coaches filled with alphabet blocks or other educational baggage usually followed the locomotive. Freight cars were almost unknown and no wooden train ever had a motor. Easily assembled by unskilled labour, light in weight, colourful and utterly harmless, these fascinating toys were highly popular and manufactured in huge volumes. Unfortunately, they suffered from being considered "suitable for infants" and the scorn older children had for them meant that few were saved for the future collector. Bliss, Reed and Milton Bradley were major manufacturers, but only Milton Bradley is still in business today, producing recognizable but far-too-bland descendants of their sharper nineteenth-century toys.

In the nineteenth century, cast iron was the plastic of its day. Skilled craftsmanship was only required for the design and execution of the dies and for the foundry work; everything else could be done by anyone right off the street, and done very quickly. Usually there were two cast iron halves which, with the wheels and axles, reduced the separate parts to a minimum. The castings could incorporate springs, rods, piping, lamps, rivets and even lettering, which resulted in a much more detailed toy at little extra cost. The parts could be dip painted and the final assembly could be done in a minute or two. The pieces illustrated left and opposite were both manufactured in this way.

Cast iron reached new heights of three-dimensional realism and some of the larger trains were very convincing miniatures. Pratt and Letchworth made an elegant New York Central and Hudson River Railway Vestibule Express pulled by the "999", the famous 4–4–0 record breaker. Over 1.5m (5ft) long, this train has always been a top collectors' prize. New York Central and Hudson

River vestibule coaches made by the Ideal Manufacturing Co. in 1896 had simulated wood sides, a truss rod underframe, accurate window framing, accurate bogie frames and an exceptionally good clerestory roof, all of which added up to the kind of scale model that would not be seen again for fifty years. Unfortunately, the locomotive that hauled these fabulous coaches was something of a caricature.

There were disadvantages with iron, such as the heavy weight and the lack of variety in the finishing – no place here for passengers with character. However, their weight lent these trains a purposeful seriousness, which was more in keeping with real trains, and undecorated black paint was the usual colour. Most of the iron trains were motorless, but by 1880 both Secor and Carpenter had patented clockwork motors for the iron trains. Ives took over Secor and marketed a wide variety of powered models. A further disadvantage was that if they broke, which they frequently did because cast iron is brittle, they stayed broken. There was no easy way to mend them. By 1900, the popularity of these trains had reached its zenith and cast iron trains were sold in diminishing numbers up until the mid-1930s.

There were three companies that made more sophisticated trains. Beggs and then Weedon both produced steam-powered trains, and Carlisle & Finch made electrically driven trains. These were toys with flanged wheels which ran on metal track. By the 1870s, Eugene Beggs was marketing, under his own name, the first American-made steam-operated toy railway set (see page 17). The gauge was 1 7/8 in (4.75cm) and the size was close to 0 scale. The locomotives had good proportions and were available in several wheel arrangements, with tenders and, as tank engines, without tenders. The painting was decorative and embellished with paint strokes, which had more to do with commercial tinware of the time than any locomotive prototype. Quite often the boilers were polished and nickel-plated. Very light coaches were available, made from cardboard bodies to which tin roofs, end platforms, steps and bogies were added. Gluing well-detailed and beautifully lithographed sides to the cardboard bodies completed the coaches. The variety of passenger and baggage coaches was quite large, and the total number of different types has been difficult to pin down. Some of the Beggs locomotives had axles set an angle to each other so that they could be run in only one direction and only on a circular track, a definite limitation to the ambitions of the junior railway magnate. Beggs trains continued to be sold until about 1906; in later years the name McNair was used, and the coaches were manufactured using lithographed tin. For a brief period, an ex-associate of Beggs named Garlick manufactured a very similar line of trains under his own name. One curiosity was a small run in

above: *A cast iron Pennsylvania Rail Road "Camelback". These trains were seldom powered and were most popular from the 1880s until about 1915.*

1895 of an extremely exotic electric locomotive with glass sides so that the electric motor could be seen.

Ten years after Beggs, in 1887, Weedon, which produced a large variety of steam toys, advertised a 2–4–0 engine, the "Dart", and an eight-wheel coach. The locomoitve was an 0–4–0 with dummy leading wheels. Slightly smaller than the Beggs locomotives, the "Dart" was still roughly 0 scale but with wheels set to a 2in (5cm) gauge. It was a charming model and quite accurate for the times, with masses of nicely embossed rivets, a huge headlamp, detailed steam chests with 1887 stamped into them, and embossed boiler details inside the cab. The coach had equally good proportions, with embossed detail that added strength, tiny lead-wheeled bogies and a clerestory roof. It was extremely light, and so the locomotive had a reasonable chance of pulling it. The rails on which it ran were usually the strip type with wooden ties. A circle or oval track was possible but not much else because no movable points, or switches, were offered. Bill Weedon himself died soon after the "Dart" was introduced and his successors made very little effort to expand on such a promising start. No accessories or additional rolling stock appeared, only a slightly larger 4–4–0, which is extremely rare today.

The most interesting firm was Carlisle & Finch of Cincinnati, Ohio, who had for sale, in 1896, a four-wheel tram running on electric track. This was the first successful electric train to be sold in the USA and was still in their catalogue in 1910. The firm expanded the line rapidly, and by 1900 there were both four-wheel and eight-wheel trams, the latter with two motors.

There was also a four-wheel mining locomotive with accompanying ore cars and an 0–4–0 steam outline locomotive, lettered for the Lake Shore and Michigan Southern Railroad. All were powered by electric motors and ran on 2in (5cm) gauge track using strip rail and wooden ties. A selection of both freight wagons and passenger coaches was offered, lettered for different American railways such as Pennsylvania, Chicago Burlington and Quincey, Union Pacific and the eponymous Electric Railway. A girder bridge was catalogued, as was a fine station with two electrically-operated signals jutting through the roof. Three types of points, or switches, and a crossover permitted the building of complex track layouts, including the ever-popular figure of eight, all in 2in (5cm) gauge. Decently long trains were possible because everything was very lightly built. The locomotives had wooden frames, which also provided a measure of insulation for the motors. Some of the decoration was embossed, but most of it consisted of printed paper glued to the tin sides of the coaches, freight cars and locomotive cabs. In the decade that followed, the success of Carlisle & Finch inspired other firms, such as Knapp and Howard, to compete with close copies of the Carlisle & Finch designs, but they were not as successful.

below: *This gorgeous French train by Maltête et Parent proves that not all the best nineteenth-century makers were German.*

FRANCE

Traditionally, French toys have predominantly been made from tin. Small pull-toys consisting of a simply designed locomotive accompanied by a couple of four-wheel coaches were made throughout the latter half of the nineteenth century. They resembled trains that were running in the 1840s: the earlier engines had no cabs, and the coaches looked as if they had bodies taken from horse-drawn carriages. Smaller ones were stamped from dies that provided a modicum of embossed detail. But the dies were rugged, and the conservative French were still producing trains well into the twentieth century that were sixty years out of date. That said, real French trains built in 1845 were still running, without much modification, in 1910.

Some of the small toys had flywheel-activated friction motors, but clockwork was reserved for the larger trains, such as the ones made by Maltête et Parent (see page 20), Jacques Caron and Dessein. These more sophisticated trains were soldered together from countless small pieces of metal by real craftsmen, carefully painted and quite magnificent. The paint had poor adhesive qualities, however, and it is very seldom that one is found with its paint intact today. Single-driver designs were favoured for their mechanical simplicity.

Lettering for all toy trains was usually in the form of printed paper showing some exciting and exotic-sounding destination such as Berlin, Paris, Marseilles, and even London. There were designations for First, Second and Third Class, and finally, notices stating whether or not smoking was permitted. These strips of paper were pasted onto the coaches just under the windows; however, they had an unfortunate habit of falling off due to failing glue.

FV, started by Edmond Faivre in 1875, is the firm responsible for the majority of the flanged-wheel, clockwork-powered trains found today. The locomotives usually have a pair of large driving wheels and a pair of small wheels and accompanying coaches in lithographed tin, a finish that began to appear in the 1880s. The rails were sectional and pressed from a single piece of tin, forming a sort of trough. No points were available, allowing only circular running, although accessories such as tunnels, stations, trees, signals and bridges added interest. FV catalogued a number of summer coaches with hand-painted passengers sitting in the open behind drawn-back curtains. Another novelty was a clockwork horse-drawn tram that ran on a track.

Most of the FV trains were 0 scale in size and the track is close to 0 Gauge. Similar trains were produced for Gauge I track, but they are almost impossible to find today. DS or Dessein, set up in 1863, made clockwork floor trains in various sizes. They are generally cabless, have a pair of driving wheels, a horizontally ribbed, gold-coloured boiler, a diamond-shaped decoration on the tender and are all hand painted.

Tanton et Manon made trains similar in size to FV but more elaborately constructed, and some of them ran on tracks similar to those used by FV. Charles Rossignol, starting up in 1868, was the longest lived of any of the French manufacturers, producing toy trains for over eighty years. The company's nineteenth-century output was entirely limited to floor runners. They were handsomely finished with brilliantly drawn and elaborate lithography, which revelled in every detail, even partially drawn blinds for the coach windows. Moreoever, Rossignol's clockwork mechanisms were marvels of simplicity and inexpensive to make.

above: *This 1890s Gauge I train by Ernst Plank looks closer in style to a nursery toy than a model railway.*

Steam-powered trains, on the other hand, were costly. Radiguet, the principal French maker, had been the leading manufacturer of scientific toys since 1872. Its locomotives were made in heavy brass and looked very much like their English counterparts, but with a more elaborate finish. These engines came in a large number of different sizes, different gauges, and with various wheel arrangements. Rails could be purchased, but most Radiguets were probably just run on the floor. Occasionally a tender was included, but rolling stock was practically non-existent.

French toy trains seemed to be made only for the French market, with no special English or German export versions, or with that added American essential, the cowcatcher. Consequently, not many French toy trains are found outside France. The French toy market, however, imported a great many trains from Germany, which dominated the European market.

GERMANY

Among the myriad German principalities, dukedoms, margraviates and the like that existed in the nineteenth century, several were renowned as toy-making centres. These were largely cottage industries, using wood or lead, although a few larger firms specialized in tinplate toys.

Lead trains were a by-product of the popular lead soldier industry, and were made by firms such as Heinrichsen of Nürnberg, Allegeyer of Fürth, and Ammon. Dies were skilfully etched into slabs of slate, into which lead was then poured to make two-dimensional but highly detailed castings, rather resembling coins. Huge armies could be produced by this method and then packed away into a fairly small space. Cannons and wagons were either flat, or made three-dimensional by soldering several flat castings together. Model boats were made this way and so were early trains, with moving wheels. The style of these trains was that of the 1840s – four- or six-wheel locomotives with no cab but with a driver and fireman, a tender, some coaches with passengers and a few freight wagons with animals. With their charming details and fine painting, these were exceptionally endearing toys (see page 10). The size was approximately HO scale, the same as the toy soldiers, the civilian figures, and the lead buildings that accompanied them (the lead boats were usually to a much smaller scale).

The casting method limited the size and, besides, larger models would have been far too flimsy. As it was, the lead trains were exceedingly fragile and it is little wonder that so few of them exist today. Examining the survivors, they all appear to be modelled after the very first trains. It is difficult to determine for how long a period they were made, but certainly they must have delighted many a child.

Erzegebirge, in rural Saxony, is famous for the wooden toys that have been made there for 300 years. Generations of peasants have made these toys around the hearth and each village has its speciality: Hallbach was the centre for arks, for instance, and Olbernhau for toy guns. Small factories also supplied turnings and semi-finished work. Although Erzegebirge toys are traditional, when trains, cars and planes appeared, their toy counterparts were added to the range and updated from time to time, so that the early cabless locomotives acquired cabs, and smoking chimneys – lots of billowing smoke was a big design feature in the early, cheap trains, both wood and lead. The small trains were sold with a surprisingly large number of coaches, each containing passengers, and the train could be

given movement by letting it roll down an inclined track. Very thin wire axles allowed free rolling, a feature that appeared a century later in Mattel's Hot Wheels range. Since people, buildings, stations, trees, horse-drawn carriages and animals were all available cheaply, manufactured to roughly the same scale, a fine railway scene could be built up that was more robust than the lead trains and could be enjoyed more fully.

The tinplate toy industry was centred on Nürnberg, where the Hess company, founded in 1826, was the first one to make floor-running trains in lightweight tinplate. The earliest Hess trains were embossed, hand-painted with floral patterns and nailed to wooden bases. From these, Hess moved on to all-tin construction with printed paper pasted to the sides for decorative detailing.

Cheap floor trains were also made by Issmayer and Günthermannn. Both firms were established in the mid-nineteenth century and moved quickly into lithographed tinplate when the techniques were sufficiently developed. Lithography provided for an immense range of colourful,

below: *A Schönner Gauge I train with typical flat-fronted smokebox and tapering chimney. Its over-sized driving wheels make it look particularly attractive.*

detailed and cheap toys, but demanded mass production to offset the high tooling costs. Tin tab construction had to be developed to replace soldering, which was slow – it is interesting to see lithographed toys that have been soldered together and speculate on the skill required to solder the parts without ruining the lithography.

Clockwork motors, specially designed for lightweight and inexpensive manufacture, powered many of these toys. Issmayer was one of the first to provide sectional track, which was stamped from a single piece of tin and was similar to the French FV track. This was improved to become two rolled tinplate rails fastened to three or four stamped ties. Several sections of this track were supplied with the train to form a circle, and the train itself had its axles set at an angle to one another to facilitate circular running. Several gauges were available, of which the most popular was 0 Gauge. It seems quite likely that Issmayer,

below: This Schönner Gauge III live-steam locomotive, c. 1900, was adapted for the American market with the addition of the prominent cowcatcher and front headlamp.

or possibly FV, invented 0 Gauge some time in the 1870s. Unfortunately, none of the brilliantly lithographed nineteenth-century Issmayer catalogues survive. However, quite a few of the colourful and densely detailed box tops have. Because they were changed regularly to reflect changes and improvements in the product line, they give us a good idea of the range of toys that were made.

The most prominent quality toymakers were Rock and Gräner (established in 1813), Lutz (1846) and Buchner and Leonard Staudt, who made low-production, hand-finished toys for those who could afford them. All these firms made elaborate floor trains, some with high-quality clockwork mechanisms. By the 1880s, Lutz was offering sectional track with some of its train sets; its 1891 catalogue has both the early single-piece type and the more modern one with rolled tinplate rails and separate ties.

In 1891 the Märklin brothers acquired controlling interest in Lutz and were ready to expand their toy range, which had until then been centred on dolls' house accessories. For the 1891 Leipzig Toy Fair, they prepared a ground-breaking railway exhibit which featured a figure-of-eight track and introduced three basic track gauges: Gauge I (48mm), Gauge II (54mm), and Gauge III (75mm). The exhibit was an enormous success and established Märklin in the toy train business. By including movable points, a crossover and a carefully thought out sectional track geometry, Märklin was able to offer a toy railway layout capable of unlimited growth and diversity of shape. Booklets were published full

of complicated track plans which could easily be put together – a move closely followed by other companies – and children soon learned that they could build their own designs just as quickly. A vast railway empire was possible at last. The trains could leave the nursery, travel down the hall and even into the living room. All that was required was more track and, perhaps, more powerful engines. Parents and nannies realized that this invasion of their living space was only temporary and that the track could be quickly taken apart and stored safely back in the toy box. Putting the track together and breaking it down again became a creative and fun part of playing with toy trains.

Märklin, through experience with dolls' houses and their contents, had learned that it could sell an infinite number of different things to fill up a dolls' house and that when it was full, another, larger dolls' house was required. The railway system was evidently another such toy, and Märklin began to manufacture countless accessories: stations, signals, tunnels, bridges, cranes, lamps, baggage carts, passengers, refreshment trolleys, coal loading bins, water pumps... the list expanded to fill large catalogues. Other manufacturers saw that, by adopting the Märklin gauge sizes, their own trains could be run on Märklin rails, and they too could join in the accessory explosion.

Two German firms were active in the design of steam-powered locomotives: Plank and Schönner. Plank developed a distinctive range of very individualistic locomotives that hauled lightweight rolling stock which used special wheels stamped from brass (see page 22). Schönner made more elaborate locomotives based on

more realistic prototypes and which usually ran in a straight line. In 1887, Schönner was marketing in the United States steamers based on American prototypes that were superior in size and design to anything made by the competition (see opposite).

By the end of the nineteenth century, toymakers were caught up in Germany's rapid industrialization, and they were looking to markets outside Germany for their excess production. Increasingly, they looked to the United States, Britain and France, and were soon designing trains especially adapted for these markets. Günthermannn made magnificent floor-running models of typical American and British locomotives in many different sizes. Issmayer and Hess produced smaller floor runners of distinctly American types during the 1890s, and Issmayer tracked train sets started to appear on American shelves (see page 32). Bing (founded 1863) followed its younger protégé, Carette, into the train market in the 1890s, both companies buying in Schönner steamers to fill out their lines. Wheels were turning and the toy railway industry was beginning to get up steam.

above: *This scarce example of a Gauge I Märklin clockwork locomotive and tender, c. 1898, is very simple in its construction.*

chapter 2

1900–1914

THE GOLDEN AGE

The beginning of the twentieth century, before the outbreak of World War I, is generally recognized as the Golden Age of toy trains, led by the power and wealth of Europe. There was a thriving market for top-quality toy trains, which usually required large rooms and considerable wealth to build up layouts. At the turn of the century, toy trains were a reflection of the current fascination with exciting developments in transport: steam trains were reaching record speeds in great comfort, motor cars were slowly criss-crossing the landscape, and the Wright Brothers were hesitantly pioneering powered flight at Kitty Hawk.

Tinplate toy-train production had reached its zenith of design and quality by 1914 and can be seen as a microcosm of the manufacturing strength and political insanity of the Old World. With a tragic irony, the factories that were turning out tinplate toys would soon be turned over to war work, providing material to attack the very countries that they had been supplying only months before.

The German toy industry was at its peak, driven by the great manufacturers such as Märklin, Bing and Carette. Almost any locomotive, coach, wagon or accessory was available. The business was largely for the home market, with the bulk of exports going to America, Britain and France, where domestic competition was undercut by low German labour rates.

Much of the impetus for growth came from Britain, where wealthy railway enthusiasts shaped a generation of accurate toys and models – in Britain an interest in model trains was seen as an acceptable pursuit for a gentleman. The potential of Britain as an export market was clear after the Paris "Exposition Universelle" of 1900. It was there that Wenman Bassett-Lowke and Stephan Bing formed a mutually beneficial business relationship and friendship that was to last for nearly forty years. Märklin subsequently aligned itself with A. W. Gamage, the central London department store that acted as retailer and wholesaler for the Märklin brothers' output.

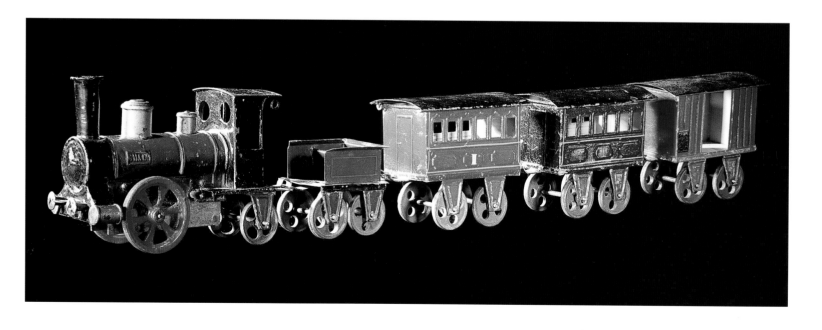

MÄRKLIN

Märklin was founded in 1859 in Göppingen, near Stuttgart, in the Swabian province of Württemberg. By 1900 it had consolidated its position as a leading quality train and toy manufacturer, using heavy-gauge tinplate – usually of Welsh origin – cut to shape, formed with the minimum of folding, then soldered and hand painted. The production philosophy of the company relied on a small but highly skilled workforce of designers, tinsmiths and painters, and Märklin models appeared almost carved from solid, although they were not always strictly accurate by comparison with the prototype.

Special locomotives, rolling stock and accessories were designed for important export markets, although in many cases these were simply domestic models adapted slightly or painted in a different style. Engines were all powered by clockwork until 1900, when safer, low-voltage electric mechanisms became available, as well as more dangerous high-voltage locomotives that could deliver a full charge in short circuit.

In 1907, Richard Safft joined the company, bringing in outside engineering experience. It was probably he who introduced new die-stamping machinery and lithography presses. Some mechanization meant that in the years up to 1914 a more diverse product range could be built up, giving free rein to the imagination – it is no co-incidence that such a vigorous company should have won the Grand Prix at the Brussels "Exposition Universelle" in 1910. The prize was won jointly with Steiff, which provided figures for the display. Steiff, based in Giengen, was not far from Göppingen, and the two companies have had a long trading friendship that still prospers.

Märklin's low cost base enabled it to produce a large variety of highly priced items of the utmost quality. Many are now of the greatest rarity. Both Märklin and Hornby issued fairly substantial catalogues in the 1920s and 1930s, but unlike the *Hornby Book of Trains*, the copiously illustrated Märklin *Hauptkatalog* was for retailers and customers to order from, not a list of what was available from stock. Many standardized parts were produced in runs for use in different models; in this way some could remain available in catalogue for over thirty years. Apart from the Sample Room, the factory stock rooms were not full of completed models; pieces were effectively built to order, often in minute quantities. It is likely that quite a number of items in Märklin catalogues were either never made at all or the tiny production run has been lost over the years. Even before World War I, the smaller 0 Gauge was becoming more popular than the larger gauges. With the advent of machine pressing and an increased range, the five-year period up to 1914 was a truly fabulous end to a golden era, tragically cut short by the careless slide into conflict. Any collector who has the good taste – and wealth – to concentrate on this area of Märklin production will never be disappointed.

Märklin and Bing stand in a class alone in terms of rarity, quality and market value today. Most collectors reading their catalogues from this period can only dream of owning many of the pieces included: page after page is filled with gems that would be the centrepiece of any toy train collection – even if some were never actually made. Their work is of such high quality and artistry that several important toy-train collectors believe that the best pieces should be classified as fine art. For Märklin, all this was achieved by a relatively small company: in 1914 it employed only 600 people, compared to 5,000 at Bing in Nürnberg.

left: *A Märklin clockwork train, c. 1895: a typical set that would have made a handsome Christmas present.*

left: *Carette's very rare electric* **Schwebebahn,** *or hanging railway, from around 1905, modelled on the original German prototype monorail that still runs today.*

The Bing brothers could not maintain the assault on Märklin's market for highly priced pieces, so they then succeeded by offering buyers a diverse range at a good price. In 1903 they took advantage of the new offset lithography drum presses to speed up and improve the quality of tinprinting. This led to the very popular "Nürnberg style" of well-detailed lighter-gauge tinplate toy railways and cheaper sets. Their output increased markedly and the number employed by the Bing brothers rose from 500 in 1895 to just over 4,000 in 1911.

Georges Carette was a French businessman and son-in-law of Ignatz Bing. He ran his own factory in Nürnberg, producing a range that mostly closely paralleled Bing's production – although it was rather more idiosyncratic. Carette used a mixture of painted and lithographed tinplate like other makers, but for locomotive components he favoured cast iron more than his competitors. Bing did use it, but mostly for stationary steam components and American-market locomotive bodies.

Like Stephan Bing, Georges Carette carried out some of his finest work under exclusive contract to Bassett-Lowke, producing rolling stock and buildings between 1910 and 1914 that showed off the art of lithography on tinplate. The detail is extraordinarily life-like – even down to the depiction of shadows on the walls of buildings. By contrast, Carette locomotive mechanisms were neither reliable nor strong. Although trading links between the two companies were severed at the outbreak of World War I, family contact remained close. Georges Carette himself returned to his native France in 1914,

BING AND CARETTE

Gebrüder Bing produced very fine toy railways in the early 1900s, combining elegance with strength, and surpassing Märklin in design, construction and paintwork. Their Gauge III locomotives were more expensive than the Märklin equivalent. Much of their best work was produced under contract to Bassett-Lowke and Gamages in Britain. The toy locomotives they produced to Henry Greenly's designs are arguably the finest ever made.

dying there in the 1920s. His partner, Paul Josephstal, took over, but the business closed in 1917 when he was called up for military service; the name passed to Richard Bauer and some of the railway tooling went to Bassett-Lowke in Northampton. A member of the family was still a shareholder in Bassett-Lowke Ltd in the 1970s.

The most unusual survival from Carette's varied and modern product range is an extremely rare example of the Wuppertaler Schwebebahn, No. 1080/2 (also modelled by Märklin) (see page 30). It was a remarkable design, with the electric motor built into one of the suspension units, and must have looked spectacular when running on its raised figure-of-eight track. Even without extension pieces, the set-up was 1.8m (6ft) long. There are probably now only three examples still surviving.

Judging from the relatively large number still seen today, Carette tramcar sets were popular at the time, with several varieties available. An oddity was a freelance South East and Chatham Railway steam railcar, No. 1601, consisting of a simple live-steam 0–4–0 side tank locomotive with a bogie coach grafted onto it.

OTHER GERMAN COMPANIES

The origins of Rock and Gräner go back to 1815. The company was based in the small town of Biberach an der Riss, in the same region as Märklin, and although it was only a cottage industry by today's standards, by the middle of the nineteenth century it was one of the largest German toymakers. Apart from making fine toy horse-drawn vehicles, Rock and Gräner produced exquisite painted tinplate dolls' house furniture and toy trains of a broadly similar style to Märklin's. The original company had been taken over in

below: *A Gauge IV Schönner Coupe-Vent locomotive and tender from 1902, based on the French "Grande C" locomotives.*

1896, so by this period the logo was R&GN, with the N standing not for Nürnberg but *Nachfolger*, meaning "successor". The company unfortunately remained too small to prosper and it closed in 1905.

In its last decade, however, Rock and Gräner was able to produce a remarkable model of the famous Armoured Train (see page 12). It is more toy-like than the rather menacing Märklin version, complete with improbably flimsy cowcatcher, and is the rarest known survival from the company's production. Rock and Gräner also produced a few pieces for the British market, which are now extremely scarce. Only one of its London and South Western Railway bogie coaches is known to exist – see opposite – and is an example of the benefits of conservative and patient restoration; when found, it had been heavily overpainted and the excess had to be removed by shaving with a scalpel and a steady hand (see page 33).

Schönner, founded by Jean Schönner in Nürnberg in 1875, had already made over half a million engines by 1893, yet apart from the ubiquitous "storkleg" and "piddler" locomotives, its products are rarely found today.

below: A lightweight clockwork train by Issmayer, c. 1900. Issmayer's gleaming gold lacquered finish on tinplate was unrivalled.

It is very probable that Schönner met Wenman Bassett-Lowke at the "Exposition Universelle" in Paris in 1900, as one of his largest models appears in the 1902 Bassett-Lowke catalogue. It is not really a set of the greatest beauty, representing in live steam Gauge III a Bavarian state railway express train. The locomotive was modelled accurately on a Maffei type B-XI; the metalwork of all the pieces seems quite plain and thin, with relatively narrow wheels, but the size and scale are certainly notable. Schönner did have problems with the priming for paint finishes, and this set is no exception; it is usually repainted, although this does not reduce its considerable value.

Even more valuable are two other fine Schönner Gauge III models pictured in the 1902 Bassett-Lowke catalogue: the elegant SECR (South Eastern and Chatham Railway) 4–4–0 Wainwright D and the PLM (Paris Lyon Méditerranée) "Grande C" Coupe-Vent (see page 31). The French outline locomotive has a lightness of touch missing from Märklin's solid version – and is worth more, even if repainted, as this one is.

Little is known about the last years of the company, but it seems to have been unable to compete against its larger rivals. The founder was also heading for retirement

age, and the firm closed between 1910 and 1912. Some production passed to Falk, another Nürnberg toy manufacturer.

The company that Johann Issmayer established early in the nineteenth century was active in exporting to America brightly coloured lightweight tinplate trains that ran on track or floors (see page 32). Issmayer specialized in very crisp lithography, using bright gold and well-lacquered bare tinplate as part of its designs; at a time when rivals produced plain card or wooden boxes, Issmayer sets were packaged with inventive labels showing bustling landscapes with its own trains in the foreground. The company also produced promotional chocolate-filled locomotives and savings banks for Stollwerck. Issmayer trains are much sought after by dedicated collectors, who can experience the aesthetic pleasures of a make happily separate from more mainstream manufacturers.

W J BASSETT-LOWKE & CO.

The history of Bassett-Lowke is intertwined with the history of Northampton. The sites of some of the old company workshops still exist today and the company is well represented in Northamptonshire County Museum, which mounted a comprehensive centenary exhibition in 1999.

The history of the company was also shaped by the character of Wenman Bassett-Lowke himself. He acquired his surname through the second marriage of his Lowke grandmother to Abraham Bassett, a boiler engineer like Wenman's father. Born in 1876, Wenman

(who preferred to be known as Whynne) set up his own business and, at 23, was selling locomotive and steam engine models through a mail-order catalogue. As a keen photographer, he made up the catalogue very economically using only his photographs rather than printed text. Unlike his contemporary, Frank Hornby, who soon after created the origins of the Meccano range, Bassett-Lowke believed in sub-contracting. Where Hornby aimed to carry out as much production work as possible in one factory, Bassett-Lowke used a complex, interrelated group of subsidiary and contracted companies spread all around Northampton.

Wenman Bassett-Lowke was fortunate to meet several loyal supporters crucial to the success of his company, set up in 1899. The first came from Northampton's long-established shoe industry – Frank Jones accompanied him to the Paris "Exposition Universelle" in 1900, where he was bowled over by the quality of German toy steam locomotives, particularly by

above: *One of the last British-market bogie coaches made by Rock & Gräner, c. 1900. It represents the London & South Western Railway.*

above: *The over-filled burner on this rare LSWR-liveried Bing Gauge II live-steam locomotive and tender from 1902 has wreaked havoc on the paintwork.*

the work of Stephan Bing and Georges Carette. Soon after the "Exposition", Bassett-Lowke met Henry Greenly, a superb technical draughtsman, and started a design relationship that lasted until 1939. Bassett-Lowke realized that Bing could produce British-out-line toy trains to Greenly's designs at lower cost and better quality than in Northampton. Between 1904 and 1914, this union produced some of the most pleasing and well-detailed locomotives to be found anywhere, making great strides from the crude British live-steam locomotives of the1890s. They combined power and accuracy, making some of the work of Märklin appear clumsy, although Märklin's products were also offered in Bassett-Lowke's catalogues.

In 1908, Bassett-Lowke and George Winteringham created a new company to design and build all types of locomotives, models and accessories of the type coming from Germany. Overall, the catalogue brought together German toy trains, specially commissioned large-gauge model garden or exhibition railways, model ships and dockyards, steam engines and small naval Waterline Models, with E.W. Twining making architectural and wooden models.

In the same year Bassett-Lowke opened his first London shop, at 257 High Holborn; two years later the business moved to 112 High Holborn, where it remained until the end of 1964, when it was taken over by Beattie's. A limited company was formed in 1910, with Jack Sears – shoe magnate and founder of Sears Holdings – as chairman; shareholders included Georges Carette and G.P. Keen, the wealthy model engineer.

Georges Carette had been a personal friend of Wenman Bassett-Lowke since the Paris Exhibition, and even after Carette's death the families stayed close; his sons remained on the share register and visited the factory as late as the 1940s. Carette supplied some of his finest work to Bassett-Lowke, and it is fitting that when his company was dissolved, much of the railway tooling went to his old friend's business.

THE BIRTH OF LIONEL

In 1901 Joshua Lionel Cowen entered the toy train market almost by accident. Trying to find a use for his recently developed, and slow-selling, electric fan motor, Cowen thought of making an electric gondola, which could be used to give some movement to shop-window displays. Shop owners liked the big 2⁷/₈in-Gauge battery-powered trains to show goods, but their customers bought them for toys – and the Lionel legend was born.

By 1905 Cowen had realized that his future was in toy trains and Mario Caruso, a young genius of an Italian engineer, joined him. The next year, 1906, was the pivotal year in Lionel history. The large and expensive 2⁷/₈in Gauge was dropped in favour of 2¹/₈in-Gauge track that used a third centre rail to carry the electricity. Of course, this was incompatible with the 2-in or 5-cm Gauge used by Carlisle & Finch, Voltamp, Knapp, Bing, Märklin and others, and in an inspired moment Cowan called his new non-standard gauge track Standard Gauge, thereby wrong-footing the competition.

The new Lionel Line was large, rugged, beautifully enamelled and had the look of value for money. For lightness and strength, all the basic shapes were made out of sheet metal, avoiding as much cast iron as possible, while simple assembly and design paid off in lower production costs. Heavy enamel paint, decorated by using inexpensive rubber stamps, looked good and avoided the large capital costs that lithography required. The Lionel Line was an upmarket, luxury product competing with the Ives Gauge I sets and the large-gauge trains of Bing and Märklin, but Cowen could offer his large trains at competitive prices. In addition to the entire new line of locomotives and rolling stock, Lionel offered a transformer that ran off the 110-volt domestic current, eliminating messy and potentially dangerous batteries.

below: *This Märklin 0 Gauge live-steam locomotive, with incorrect tender, has the burner beneath the cab.*

There was no clockwork, with its suggestion of cheap wind-ups, no steam with its attendant danger of fire – only modern, clean electricity.

The line had a steam-outline locomotive, available as a 0–4–0 or a 4–4–0 with beautiful thin-rimmed driving-wheels, which were later made thicker for strength; the thin-rimmed version is more desirable. Tenders varied, but the 0–4–0 generally had four-wheeled tenders and the 4–4–0 had larger eight-wheel tenders. These locomotives remained in production until the mid-1920s. Black with red trim was the usual finish, but specials were available in polished brass and nickel.

above: *A carefully preserved example of a 1904 Märklin Gauge I CE1021 clockwork locomotive and tender shows how realism had improved in only a few years.*

A basic selection of freight cars was also introduced in 1906, all eight-wheelers. A flat car, gondola, cattle car, tank car, side-opening ballast car, boxcar and a caboose were all included in the range but, oddly enough, no refrigerator car. Two eight-wheel Pullman cars were catalogued in 1906 but none was actually produced until 1910, so the early Lionel trains hauled freight and relied on trams to move passengers.

Trams had been good sellers in the 2 7/8in Gauge and Lionel introduced no fewer than three different trams in 1906, two different sizes of four-wheelers and eight-wheelers. A large variety, including open summer types and inter-urbans, was produced until 1916, when suddenly all trams were dropped, never to reappear.

The line gradually expanded and, with the exception of trams, the 1906 range continued, with minor changes, for the next two decades. Passenger cars were introduced in 1908 and electric-outline locomotives in 1910, along with a range of smaller-size freight cars (but still no refrigerator car). All the four-wheel and eight-wheel Lionel electric locomotives were variations of the New York Central S3 locomotive that hauled trains into Grand

Central Station. Catalogues began to be oriented to customers rather than dealers and rapidly grew into the great Lionel colour catalogues that were the envy of the industry.

MÄRKLIN LOCOMOTIVES

It is always a thrill for a toy train enthusiast to come across any Märklin locomotive from the Golden Age, rare or not; even the relatively common ones are small masterpieces. Each tinplate component was hand formed and soldered together by skilled tinsmiths, then spray-primed and hand-painted by a succession of painters, with a session in the oven between each coat. The best painters, usually women, undertook the last and most complicated phases of detailed paintwork and lining. Finally, the pieces were coated with a natural shellac lacquer and baked again. These processes combined to give the thick, lustrous finish, surpassed only by Bing at its peak.

The variety of models available in this period was immense. At one end of the scale, Märklin produced many thousands of simple four-wheel clockwork locomotives between 1894 and 1902. Usually painted black or dark green, they had tall cabs open to the elements, large red wheels, high splashers, tall funnels, large steam domes and tiny tenders (see page 25). Their spindly, elongated appearance resembled the curious creations of Rowland Emmett, the famous British cartoonist with *Punch* magazine in the 1940s and 1950s, who depicted elderly drivers nursing ancient steam locomotives along crumbling causeways.

At the other end of the scale, around 1906 Märklin manufactured perhaps a dozen Gauge V (120mm) live-steam locomotives and passenger coaches for the British and American markets. They were

below: *This very unusual Märklin 0 Gauge van cunningly conceals behind sliding doors the clockwork mechanism that aids locomotives on a long haul.*

primarily intended as prodigy pieces, serving to display the consummate skill of Märklin as toymakers. As locomotive and tender together were 135cm (53in) long, they certainly succeeded in being eye-catching (see page 55).

Märklin had standardized the track and gauge system with their display at the Leipzig Toy Fair in 1891. They also helped to popularize wheel flanges and self-contained sets with track, so that trains could now run in a prescribed manner rather than heading off across the floor in an aimless and unguided meander.

Early locomotives tend to have bolder and simpler detailing, with more exaggerated and unrealistic features. The company logo, GM, was embossed into the smoke-box door and GM&Co appeared in a panel on the side of the boiler. Later, in the years just before 1914, the smokebox door was plain, and, instead, an orange GM shield was rubber-stamped on the underside of the pieces. Couplings that, early on, were simple, large ovoid loops and hooks had, by 1909, evolved into the universal lifting and sliding drop-link box coupler that remained in service until 1954.

right: *A Bing Gauge IV live-steam locomotive and tender No. 164/590, built between 1909 and 1915. It was an expensive piece when new, rivalling Märklin in its hefty build.*

The typical workhorse steam locomotive of the early twentieth century was of an 0–4–0 (B) or 4–4–0 (2B) wheel arrangement, which Märklin clothed in a huge variety of body styles. German liveries were usually green or black with red wheels, with straw or red lining and sometimes both; they were often highlighted with painted rivet detail that was sometimes embossed into the tinplate as well. Some popular early lines stayed in the catalogue for many years, alongside more modern examples; details such as couplings are the easiest clue to dating.

With a few cost-effective additions or alterations, these same steam locomotives were then sold into export markets, principally the USA and Britain. American pieces acquired cowcatchers soldered to the front buffer beam, bells on top of the boilers, large square-section cabs and, sometimes, stovepipe chimneys. British locomotives were usually painted in the liveries of the most popular railway companies: green for the Great Northern, black for the London and North Western, crimson lake for the Midland Railway or apple green for the London and South Western.

Despite the good quality of Märklin "workhorse" locomotives of this period, they can be surprisingly affordable today, particularly when compared with the huge sums of money that can be spent on very rare or top-of-the-range pieces. Thus pieces with the special deep and treacly Märklin finish can be collected at reasonable outlay, although they are still hard to find in excellent condition – not only are they now around a century old, but simpler train sets tend to be more heavily played with. Damage and wear will reduce value considerably, and it is not worth buying pieces that are badly worn or incomplete, unless they are very cheap or very rare.

POWER

Some early steam mechanisms in locomotives were alarming, originating with the No. 4020 of 1898, which used a spirit tank under the cab roof, firing a jet of flame into the open heat trough in the centre of the boiler – lethal when knocked over. In later locomotives this projectile had been tamed with a conventional vaporizing spirit burner under the cab (see page 35).

Clockwork mechanisms were at least safe, but they were tiresome to use, however strong their springs. In

1908 Märklin devised an ingenious solution to the problem of repeated winding. The sliding doors of the SK1020 "Special-Kraftwagen" or power car, apparently a goods van of plain appearance, opened to reveal an extra motor (see page 37), and the unusually large wheels were powered to act as a surreptitious banking engine.

Electric mechanisms were far more convenient, but few family homes at the time had electricity supplies. Coming from different private generating companies, electricity could be direct, alternating or three-phase current. The high-voltage versions (110–250 volts) could transmit the full voltage through the unfortunate user if the variable resistor was short-circuited, so electric lamp bulbs were used as basic step-down transformers; in typically careful fashion, Märklin sometimes enclosed them in little houses. It also introduced safe but less powerful 4-volt electromagnet and 4-volt and 8-volt permanent magnet mechanisms.

BING LOCOMOTIVES

Some Bing clockwork hand-painted 0–4–0 locomotives from the turn of the century are similar in appearance to Märklin products, but they are distinguished by having the initials GBN – which stands for Gebrüder Bing, Nürnberg – ornately embossed on the smokebox door.

The company's 1902 catalogue gives a good indication of Bing's range. The most basic were the 2–2–0 *Storchbein* or "storkleg" locomotives, with simple oscillating cylinders that connected directly to the oversize driving wheels, without any form of valve guides or coupling rods. More sophisticated versions, at over twice the price, had fixed cylinders and jointed connecting rods. Twice as much money would buy you the live-steam Gauge II 4–4–0 locomotive No. 7090/2, with tender, but this was still inexpensive compared with the Gauge III home-market version of the freelance 7093/3 "Black Prince" 4–4–0.

The catalogue also included just a small number of pieces for the American market that are, consequently, very rare today. The locomotive in the Gauge I 7113/0

set was redesigned to include cowcatcher, large headlamp above the smokebox and bell, bogie dining car and sleeping car; together the set is of a quality that surpasses Märklin.

By 1908 the range for the home market had become plainer in style, typified by a new Gauge I 0–4–0 steam locomotive and tender, No. 9643/1. It had a plain splasher over the driving wheels, a streamlined smokebox and simply lined four-wheel tender; despite appearances, there was not a wheel set missing from the middle of the tender.

A much more substantial Gauge IV live-steam locomotive and tender was available from 1909 to 1915. No. 164/590 (see page 39) approached the Märklin "Württemburg" in scale and grandeur and represented some of the finest work to come from Gebrüder Bing just prior to World War I. The large driving wheels and high splashers gave it a purposeful appearance and some modern streamlining to the cab softened its form. It was an expensive piece, and few were sold, making it very rare today.

above: *This beautifully detailed American-market Bing Gauge I clockwork 4–4–0 from 1902 marks a brief time when Bing surpassed Märklin in quality and price.*

PASSENGER ROLLING STOCK

Märklin's typical Gauge I four-wheel or two-axle coach from this period is 12cm (4³/4in) long and very toy-like, with oversized wheels, small body and plain panelled sides, painted in red, blue and green (see page 28). This was part of the equivalent of a "starter set"; it usually accompanied the basic green 0–4–0 locomotive and tender, which also hauled the next size up, at 15cm (6in) long. The larger coach was modelled with more detail, including dummy doors, more realistic springs and dimples for roof ventilators. Both are still affordable for collectors today. The larger size, at 20cm (8in) long, allowed for opening doors, hinged roofs, clerestory roofs and running boards; it is far more highly valued.

An oddity from 1902 worth hunting for – but rarely seen – appears to be just a humble four-wheel coach but is, in fact, the aptly named Katastrophewagen (No. 1837). The only obvious clue to its function is an overlong buffer: when carelessly shunted, it releases a sprung pin

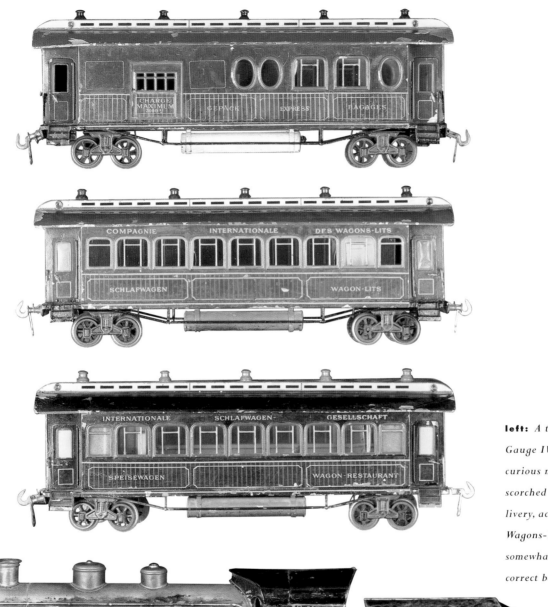

left: *A top-of-the-range Bing Gauge IV train set, with a curious mixture of a rather scorched locomotive in LNWR livery, accompanied by Wagons-Lits coaches with somewhat undersized but correct bogies.*

above: *A Gauge I bogie dining car from 1898, at the peak of Bing's quality production. It is harder to find coaches of this type than the Märklin equivalent.*

that causes the roof to fly off and the sides to explode in a shower of different components.

The next jump was to bogie or four-axle coaches. These were usually 28.5 or 29cm (about 11¼in) long and the most renowned examples from this period are also reasonably easy to find: they were known as "Kaiser" cars because some versions were emblazoned with a golden crown, representing a vehicle from the Imperial train. The earliest type had very plain bogie frames and wheels and window openings were either squared-off double panes or arched-top single panes. All were fitted with clerestory roofs and some with interiors. They were usually hand painted in green, blue or red, neatly lined, with imitation curtains and windows on the opening vestibule doors. Kaiser cars in Märklin's 1902 catalogue had updated bogie frames and

wheels (see opposite) and were still in the 1909 catalogue as a variation of the No. 1840 series, with more modern bogies, coach sides and roof ventilators.

The new investment imported by Richard Safft resulted in updated designs. No. 1847, the very desirable "Süd Express" bogie coach in blue livery (see page 44) featured real glass windows, detailed interior, three opening doors on each side, hinged fall-plates to cover the gaps between coaches and optional flexible corridor connectors. Two other new models accompanying this coach were the green bogie Post and Baggage Van (No. 1844) and the brown bogie Baggage Van with raised guard's roof lookout and tail lights (No. 1846). Both are beautifully painted, with detailed interior fittings.

A more modern range of Gauge I Wagons-Lits coaches appeared in Bing's 1912 catalogue. Both the Restaurant Car (No. 10827/1) and the Sleeping Car (No.

10228/1) are hand painted in fragile mottled brown, with fitted interiors. By now the bogies are more realistic and well detailed and the bodies are closer to scale length.

A pretty 1902 curiosity in Bing's range was the Gauge I four-wheel Summer or Observation car (No. 7088/1). It was used on mountain or rack railways, with the open veranda giving passengers panoramic views of the surrounding landscape. It is much sought after by collectors, although it is the wrong gauge for the inexpensive rack railway that Bing introduced in 1908. Another unusual piece from 1902 is Bing's version of the Kaiser car, with elaborate Gothic windows and embossed metal crowns – Märklin could only run to transfers.

Bassett-Lowke imported a range of Bing stock, much of it in the form of four-wheel passenger coaches in the principal British railway liveries. Early Bing imports were elaborate eight-wheelers in Gauges 0, I, II, III and IV, all with detailed interiors. These were the finest coaches ever

made for the British market, but they were too heavy for the underpowered locomotives. Much of the "home-grown" stock was hand-built in painted wood at great cost; although it was very expensive at the time, it tends to age badly and is now popular with only a relatively small number of collectors.

Carette's unrivalled skill in lithography on tinplate was shown off in its rolling stock, with some of the finest lithography reserved for British-market stock for Bassett-Lowke. It was achieved in an unostentatious way, simply emphasizing detail and realism, while keeping the weight to a minimum. The LNWR suburban clerestory-roof Passenger Carriage lacked only a layer of soot to make it look absolutely realistic. On a more elevated plane, the 1910 Bassett-Lowke catalogue shows a model of the latest LNWR Dining Car, equipped with modern features such

below: *Produced from 1898 to 1909, Märklin's popular Kaiser cars were hand painted and emblazoned with the imperial crown. This model dates from around 1902.*

as smooth-running six-wheel bogies and an elliptical roof. Carette here has achieved a lightness of touch missed by other makers. The top-of-the-range Carette coaches were the hand-painted Gauge I bogie Pullmans from 1903. The No. 135/4/48 Sleeping Car (see opposite) included a fitted interior, roof ventilators, opening doors and detailed bogies.

above: *Top of the range in 1909, this royal blue Märklin "Süd Express" bogie coach has three opening doors on each side.*

FREIGHT ROLLING STOCK

Most of Märklin's early freight wagons were built around a simple four-wheel chassis, with oversized wheels. The 1902 catalogue shows typical stock, such as the Goods Van, Open Wagon and Cattle Truck, which are still very affordable. It also shows special-purpose vehicles such as the Petroleum Tank Wagon, Gas Cylinder Wagon for coach lighting, Crane Wagon, Covered Wagon with "Staats Eisenbahn" tilt and tipping wagon. More sought after is the Beer Wagon, with a colourful transfer of the "Münchener Kindl" emblem, and the Tar Wagon. More expensive were the Ambulance Wagon, complete with

stretcher case, the Service Wagon with open rear deck, and the Snow Plough with its bulky grey plough blade at the front. The composition figures of the crew stood behind stiffly to attention, protected from the impending snow cascade only by a large lamp at the front; the lamp and crew are often replaced replicas.

Bogie wagons were not well represented in the 1902 catalogue, but it did include the rare Ambulance Wagon, as well as some very sought-after pieces – the vehicle transporter wagons. These were low-sided open wagons carrying horse-drawn road vehicles – No. 2177 Deutsche Möbel Transport Gesellschaft (furniture removal) and No. 2178 Circus Van. Later renumbered No. 1877 and No. 1878, these were joined in 1909 by the even rarer No. 1879 Circus Cage Wagon available in various guises, including Circus Oriental, Cirque Russe, Cirque Américain and Carl Hagenbeck's Menagerie, the most famous European circus of its day.

A novel four-wheel wagon was introduced in 1906 that appeared deceptively simple. The Heizwagen (heating wagon, No. 1869/1) appears similar to a work break van with a raised central roof section, but on opening the double doors a complex burner with steam pipes is revealed, which actually produces steam to keep adjacent passenger coaches warm. The last example (see page 46) fetched well over £10,000 at auction in 1999.

Another rare vehicle, introduced in 1907, is completely different in character. This is the "Gefangenen Wagen" or prison van (No. 2993/1). The small barred windows give a clue to the grim interior – which is fitted with four bleak tinplate cells for prisoners in transit, with guards' seats and tables outside.

A modern transport phenomenon was introduced in 1908 – the aeroplane. A flat wagon was fitted with locating tabs and wire rails each side so that it could be used as a plane transporter. It could accommodate a dismantled tinplate model of a single-engined Blériot-type monoplane, its Spartan appearance a reminder of the

bravery of the aviation pioneers. This was an expensive toy when it was new, selling for more than double the price of a comparable plain wagon. As it was made for many years without any change to the design, it can be bought relatively cheaply today, especially since it is often found with a replica aeroplane.

In keeping with other tooling developments, the 1909 catalogue shows the rare Car Transport Wagon No. 1923. It came complete with motor car, a miniature red-painted open tourer, which has almost always been replaced by a replica (see page 47). Expensive when new in the same year was the magnificent No. 1915/1 "Talbot" bogie Hopper Wagon (see page 48). It was so hefty that it appeared to be solid, and was designed to self-discharge ballast for permanent way work.

below: *One of the finest hand-painted Carette coaches is this bogie Pullman Sleeping Car from 1903, which came with fitted interior and realistic bogie detailing.*

above: *The extremely rare 1906 Märklin steam "Heizwagen" (heating wagon), which permitted real steam to be piped into the passenger coaches for maximum realism.*

right: *The rather grim Märklin prison van from 1907 is usually found with French inscriptions.*

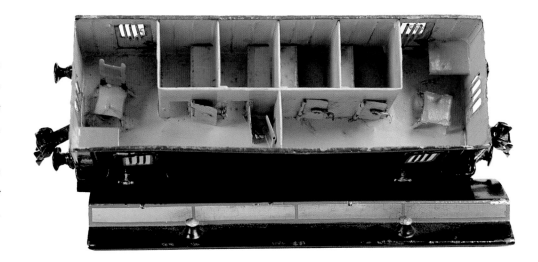

top: *From Märklin's 1906 catalogue: K.A.C. was a German motoring club and this pretty blue wagon usually contained an attractive red motor car.*

left: *This clockwork-powered crane from 1905 is the scarcest one Märklin produced and is valued accordingly.*

above: *The 1909 Talbot-system Hopper Car, decorated with hundreds of Märklin's painted rivets.*

Bing presented a range that paralleled the rival production from Märklin, including goods vans, open wagons, tank wagons, beer vans, fish vans, coal wagons and brake vans. Of the brake vans there survives only one example of an unusual variation for which Bing used the same pressing for both sides of the van, so the guard is looking out of the back on one side and the front on the other. Bing's rare No. 9193 Furniture Transport Wagons (see opposite), which clearly followed the same prototype as the Märklin equivalent, were still in the 1906 British-market catalogue. Some early British-market freight vehicles are rare, such as the Cycle Van, a reflection of the popularity of touring by bicycle at the beginning of the last century.

Carette used to put "I 48" somewhere on its vehicles, to show the gauge. The No. 134/85/48 "Ledererbräu Nürnberg" Beer Wagon from its 1914 catalogue looks quite humble, until close inspection shows that the van destination blackboard at one end has "I 48" written on it, as if by a miniature hand.

MÄRKLIN TRAMCARS, UNDER-GROUND AND RACK RAILWAYS

At the turn of the nineteenth and twentieth centuries, many people saw a successful future for street and tram cars in the battle against traffic congestion; ironically, the motor car was seen in 1900 as a liberation from the smell and mess of the ubiquitous horse. Keeping abreast of modern technology, Märklin modelled several of these new vehicles; today they look naïvely quaint, adding to their popularity.

From 1900 onwards, Märklin produced variants of four- and eight-wheel tramcars with either clockwork or electric mechanisms (see page 50), although most were titled Electrische Strassenbahn (electric tramway). The early four-wheel models were brightly coloured, with simple coachwork and open veranda ends for driver and passengers; by 1904 they were becoming more substantial and by 1907 were fully enclosed. The most elaborate was the early eight-wheel No. 3441 Electrische Schnellbahn or S-Bahn from 1903, which was based on a full-size passenger coach powered by overhead catenary wires. Its successor, No. S3081, came with underslung motor and two trailer cars, one of which had interior lighting. The accompanying No. 2629 Wartehalle (tram shelter), from 1904 is very rare; at only 26cm (10in) long, it looks more like a refreshment kiosk but is a vital complement to a complete tram layout.

The Dampfmotorwagen was an oddity that turned out to be a dead end in the advance of transport technology. In English it would be called a steam tram, but in German it was also known as a Serpolletwagen, after the French designer Léon Serpollet. A contemporary of Armand Peugeot and Louis Renault, Serpollet was vehemently opposed to the internal combustion engine; for posterity, his name has survived in Märklin No. 4041, an attractive 0–2–4 vehicle constructed from a clerestory-roof bogie coach, with the front bogie replaced by a small vertical steam engine with centre chimney and cylinders tucked up close to the front steps.

The world's first underground railway line was built in London, opening on 10 January 1863, so it is appropriate that the first Märklin underground locomotive was modelled on a four-wheel Central London Railway prototype. It appeared just a year after the actual line had been opened by the Prince of Wales and was issued as No. V1021 in clockwork form and V3021 with high-voltage electric motor. It had the typical outside motor frame of the period, but this was

below: *Furniture vans in two sizes, from Bing. These date from about 1904–1906.*

ELECTRIC TRAMWAY

hand painted in lined bright red. It had sliding doors with dummy painted glazing above the window apertures and was fitted with clockwork or high-voltage motors, ingeniously slung under the floor with an annular gear to one bogie (see page 52).

Even rarer than British underground trains are American streetcars. A high-voltage version, running number 320, was produced in 1902 with sliding doors and domed windows. No. A3190 was an eight-wheel bogie streetcar made specifically for the American market, finished in red and brown; it had inward-opening doors at each end and is known only as an unpowered car (see page 53). There is also an uncatalogued Third Avenue streetcar in 0 Gauge or Gauge I, painted in orange and brown, which was manufactured in 1914–1919.

After great and rapid labour, the Paris Métro opened on 19 July 1900, just in time for the great Exposition Universelle. Märklin briefly issued a two-car Métro set as No. 3190 in 1908–9 (see page 52), which caught the boxy appearance of the original, with decorative lining embellishing the Gauge I version.

Switzerland is home to the largest number of rack railways in the world, although the idea was actually patented in Britain in 1811 by John Blenkinsop, as a horizontal railway at Middleton Colliery in Leeds. The first Swiss mountain rack railway was the Vitznau Rigi Bahn in the Swiss canton of Luzern, which opened in 1871.

Märklin adopted two different systems. The first used a simple 0 Gauge electric locomotive, No. 3320L, with the rack outside the running rail; the second used the more sophisticated No. 2320 locomotive with inside rack. The locomotives are plainly finished in black and are

enclosed in the stubby "steeplecab" bodywork, which resembled a glazed wardrobe with a little bonnet at each end. It was hand painted in deep blue, with the usual oversize rivet detail, and was accompanied by a handsome No. 1821 four-wheel coach hand painted in blue and cream and lettered "Central-London". Its sister locomotive, No. CL3021, nearly half as long again at 32.5cm (12³/₄in), was issued in 1903 (see opposite) and is considerably more elongated, with two bogies and a small pair of doors on each side. Both locomotives are now very hard to find.

Between 1906 and 1910 a two-car District Railway train, No. 2450 or 2451, was available with a special body

above: *Märklin's electric trams made convenient use of the company's four-coupled electric motor. Unfortunately, these trams are easy to fake, using a coach body.*

very collectible. Far more interesting, however, are two special coaches. The smaller was a Summer Car (No. 1825) that definitely had sunny days in mind; the only weather protection is five curtains down each side, neatly gathered in delicately painted tinplate. The larger coach, No. 1824, is an Observation Coach, with a side corridor open to the elements and decorative gallery with scroll-work above. The rarest accessory of all is the High Level Station (No. 2034), 66cm (26in) high, with twin staircase towers flanking the raised permanent way, complemented by rugged mountains made from wood and painted plaster, some nearly 3m (10ft) in length.

HISTORIC TRAINS

Between 1906 and 1909, Märklin offered a live-steam train set hauled by the most famous of all the pioneer British steam locomotives – George and Robert Stephenson's "Rocket". From the very small number of examples that are known to have survived, it does not seem to have sold in large numbers, despite the distinguished history of the prototype (see page 14). Märklin's model was 81cm (32in) long and the designers achieved a fair resemblance to the original. It captures well the stovepipe chimney, although as a centre-flue boiler it emerges too high from the front; the cab is bracingly open and the cylinders are mounted at about the right angle. The wheels are too small and mounted inboard, but if they had been modelled to scale the boiler would have been so small that it would not have steamed adequately. The tender looks realistic and the train appears suitably basic. One carriage is simply a production four-wheel type with the roof left off. Collectors would not let a few inaccuracies deter

below: *The Central London Railway loco-motive from 1903 was usually produced by Märklin in an incorrect dark blue. Brown, red and green examples have also been found.*

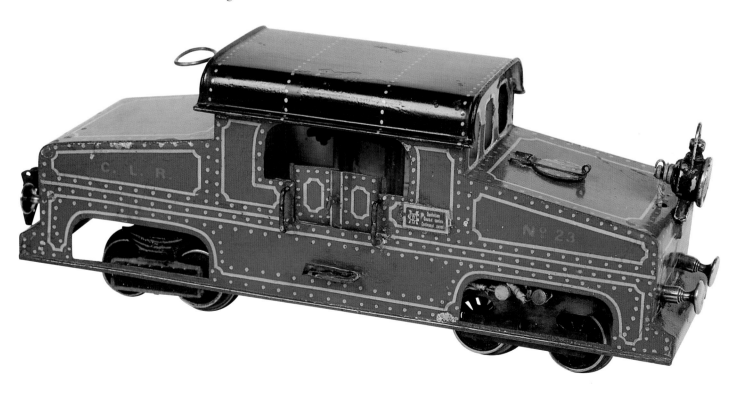

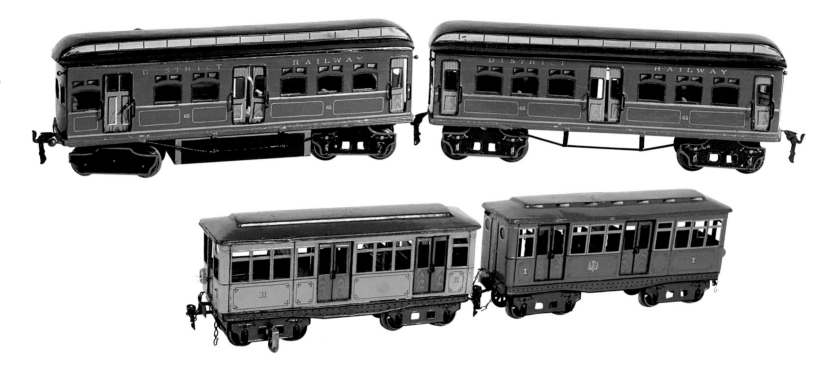

top: *This Märklin District Line London Underground train, powered by clockwork through an ingenious annular gear, was available from 1906 to 1910.*

above: *The French Métro set made by Märklin from 1908 to 1909. It had two or three cars and, logically, was powered by electricity.*

them from paying a huge amount of money to own one.

The Wuppertaler Schwebebahn, or Hanging Railway, looks like something that Jules Verne could have created, but the prototype really exists, as a working monorail in the Wupper Valley in Germany. The original, which was opened on 1 March 1901, was designed by Carl Eugen Langen and winds for 13km (8 miles) between the towns of Barmen and Elberfeld. It has carried over 1.5 billion passengers. The cars run under a rail suspended from girders that are supported in turn by 944 huge U-shaped beams. Unlike the Carette model (see page 30), the Märklin version of the Schwebebahn (No. 2341) is clockwork. It runs on extended figure-of-eight rail hanging from eight huge

supports and the whole unit is nearly 2.5m (8ft) long overall. Only a handful exist today.

Another oddity, the "Draisine" (No. 2431) or Rail Inspection Car (see page 8), relied on a simpler motive force – manpower. The rail inspector would sit in comfort, flanked by two warning flags, while two men behind him operated the crank handle; their elaborate uniforms reflected the status of the German railway system as an offshoot of the army. Its toy counterpart, modelled to a very large scale, is driven by a powerful clockwork motor that turns two oversized wheels and a cam which moves the handle backwards and forwards. The men's arms are made of fabric, which allows the mechanism to move freely. This curious and appealing vehicle is a rare survivor with its figures intact; being made of fabric and painted composition, the men are extremely vulnerable to fading and damage.

Keeping faith with modern events, the 6021 Armoured Train appeared in the 1902 catalogue, bristling with weaponry for its trip across the nursery floor. The prototype had just seen service with British troops in the Anglo-Boer War, which broke out in 1899. On 15 November it was making one of its regular excursions from the town of Estcourt when it was ambushed by the Boers; in the ensuing battle 58 men were captured, including a young journalist by the name of Winston Churchill. The model consisted of a clockwork 0–4–0 locomotive and tender with armoured casings for each, and four armoured wagons – one propelled in front, with two cannon protruding, two covered and one open, for the less fortunate; all were equipped with a vicious array of rifle slits and cap-firing mechanisms within. The armour plating was represented by heavily riveted black-painted frames supporting grey panels.

The 4023W Gauge III "Württemburg" 4–4–0 Locomotive and Tender – or "Extra Grosse" – was the largest and most powerful practical live-steam locomotive produced by Märklin (see page 5); it first appeared in the 1913 catalogue. The "Württemburg" was built to a larger scale than the usual Gauge III locomotives and many of its hefty components were constructed of cast iron. A large tender tank and feed-water pump were provided to supply the huge boiler. The smokebox door was even fitted with an electric headlight which was operated from a battery in the tender. The cab's lines were smoothed to follow the latest streamlined "wind-cutter" designs, but no finesse in detailing could completely disguise the bluff front buffer beam and colossal cylinder chests.

below: *Unpowered Gauge I Third Avenue New York street car, made by Märklin in 1914. These street cars were uncatalogued, although a couple of 0 Gauge examples have been found with electric motors.*

MÄRKLIN SPECIAL LOCOMOTIVES AND TRAINS

Imagination and diversity are two of the keys to the remarkable work Märklin achieved before World War 1. Only the most fortunate or persistent collectors are likely to own more than one or two items of this calibre – they are all of extraordinary rarity and value. The last digit of Märklin reference number refers to the gauge of the piece, usually 0, 1 or 2.

The Henschel Kassel–Hannover locomotive

One of the rarest of all Märklin locomotives was only available in 1904, at the same time as the prototype – another monument to engineering eccentricity. In 1902–3, a competition was held to produce a new design of powerful locomotive capable of 150 kmh (93mph). The Prussian firm of Henschel & Sohn, founded in Kassel in 1848, responded with a 2' B 2' (4–4–4) three-cylinder streamlined design with bogie tender, put forward by the engineers Wittfeld and Kuhn.

❶

Two versions of these unusual Kassel–Hannover locomotives were built with cabs at both ends to improve ergonomics. Despite their advanced appearance and record speed of 137kmh (81mph), they did not perform to specification and were withdrawn.

Märklin chose to model the locomotive (No. KH4021) as a live-steam streamlined cab-forward locomotive without tender. It is a curious creature, with distinctive arrow-shaped nose and slab sides, the sombrely painted plating enlivened by rivet detail, pierced windows and opening doors. The model was made in minute quantities, and probably only four or five exist today; as a live-steam locomotive they are prone to firing damage.

The Gauge V Train

The small range of Gauge V pieces produced by Märklin in around 1906 were really "prodigy" pieces, intended as display items to show off the quality and scale of production possible from the Göppingen factory. Using the same basic design, they were adapted for each of the principal export markets: in black LNWR or GNR livery for the British market and with full cab, straight splashers, bell and cowcatcher for the American market. They never appeared in catalogues and were supplied to major department stores.

With a 120mm (4 3/4in) gauge and a scale of approximately 1:12, the track for these enormous trains would only fit into palatial accommodation and it is unlikely that most had a hard working life. The few surviving locomotives simply look like Gauge II or III models enlarged to a monumental scale. They require a litre (1 3/4 pints) of methylated spirits to fill the burner and a small stationary engine in the cab to drive the feed-water pump from tender to boiler.

The passenger coaches are more remarkable than the simply detailed locomotives. With the freer hand of a large scale, normal Märklin features have been exaggerated to almost sculptural dimensions: generous seats with button backs look invitingly comfortable, and there are luggage racks and coat hooks. The dining car includes a well-fitted kitchen but, curiously, no dining tables. The smoking car is lit by three ornate gasoliers and furnished with six wickerwork bergères and two sofas. An American-market example in fair condition, with over 60m (200ft) of track, sold at Christie's in December 2001 for £113,750.

1 This Märklin Henschel Kassel–Hannover locomotive, clearly showing the forward control cab and lack of tender, dates from 1904.

2 The "Gardiner" Märklin Gauge V train, named after the family that bought it new from FAO Schwarz in around 1906.

ACCESSORIES

It is no surprise that toy-train manufacturers comple-mented their range of locomotives and rolling stock with lineside accessories, from stations and tunnels to platform clocks and ticket machines – the 1909 Märklin catalogue included 32 pages of buildings and accessories. Among the most dramatic are the large bridges, including the rare No. 2513 clockwork swing bridge. Even tinplate tunnels are elaborately embossed with stone entrances, rocky ridges and paths, and decorated with castles, chapels, houses or reservoirs.

The most frequently found early Märklin station is No. 1941 from 1900–02, known as the "Turkish Bath". It is relatively simple in form, but well decorated, with anthemion pressings along the eaves and acid-etched glass in the windows. The larger Onion Dome Station, No. 2004, was produced for longer, from 1895 to 1909, but is more sought after by collectors.

The No. 02014 Station from 1902 was more modern and accurate in appearance, with embossed stonework and roof tiling and an awning to one side protecting tables and chairs. The small but neat revised No. 02014 Town

right: *In 1904 Märklin developed an entire range of stations based on this handsome stamping. This is a particularly elaborate example, with a café and dormer windows.*

Station with Side Café was introduced in 1904, incorporating a great deal on a base only 42cm (17in) long

Some of the best Märklin buildings copy those put up for special purposes, such as the No. 2133 Customs House from 1904 (see page 60). On a more basic level, the No. 2598 Ladies and Gentlemen's Lavatory served a vital function. The toy version comes complete with fully fitted interiors finished in tasteful pink, with locking doors (see page 59). A Post Office, Signal Cabins and various station buffets were also modelled.

In general, Bing buildings are not as popular with collectors as similar Märklin examples, but still have special qualities that set them apart. Brickwork was modelled in a lighter fashion, using crisper pressings and less glutinous paint. The No. 13183 Station, introduced in 1909, had an entirely lithographed façade and narrow roof behind, unlike any Märklin product.

In 1912, Bing introduced the No. 10236 Station, probably their best-selling large model, as it remained in catalogue until 1928. They proudly announced that the walls represented imitation sandstone, and the whole piece does look impressive, at 59cm (23in) long, with lithographed door and window details and towers flanking the entrance (see page 58).

Apart from tunnels and bridges, one of the largest Bing accessories was the No. 14478 Tower Crane, introduced in 1909 – ideal for unloading wagons. Bing also produced a diverse group of island platforms, canopies, goods sheds, engine sheds, crossing-keeper's cottages and level crossings. Smaller accessories included trolleys, lamps, destination indicators, signals and warning bells; one of the most appealing is the Newstand from 1902 that gleams like a small jewel (see page 58).

The painting on it is so thick and the detail so thorough that it outdoes a Märklin product.

Like Märklin and Bing, Carette produced an equivalent variety of stations, bridges, signals, tunnels, cranes and lineside accessories. As with their freight stock, some of the finest pieces were made for the British market, such as the "brick-built" Water Tower, visible behind the Märklin "Cock o' the North" on page 97.

From the same period, 1913, comes an accessory of almost photographic realism – the Country Station made by Carette for Bassett-Lowke. Although modelled on Harrow Station, it was treated as a generic design and can

above: *This Märklin Weighbridge featured tracks for both Gauge I and 0 Gauge. The scale actually worked.*

above: *Available from 1912 to 1928, this large and popular Bing station was painted with lithographed door and window decorations. The tower tops are lead castings, which are frequently missing.*

top right: *The ever-popular Märklin lavatory from 1909, which featured advertisements for other Märklin toys.*

right: *Bing's extremely desirable 1902 newstand. It is lettered in English, French and German and came with tiny newspapers.*

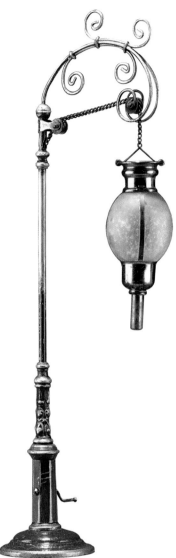

above: *Märklin lamps like this were lit by a wick, using fuel from a reservoir under the bulb – not a safety toy. They were available for many years.*

left: *This Märklin signal cabin contains switches for operating electric accessories. It was in the catalogue for a short time before World War I.*

Zoll- Revision

Ausgang

above: *The Märklin Customs House of 1904 was to be used for border-crossing toy railways. Only a couple of examples are known to have survived.*

be found identified as Clapham Junction, Four Oaks and Beaconsfield. It is very hard to find in good condition; as with Hornby, windows are represented by lacquered tinplate, so are very vulnerable to damage, and the station name boards and lamps are often missing. The accompanying water tower is also rarely found in good condition.

SUPPLYING THE BRITISH MARKET

Bing was the principal supplier of locomotives to Bassett-Lowke (see page 33) before World War I. A combination of the constructional skills of Bing and the designs of Henry Greenly proved so successful that most were reissued after

the war and some were current right up until Bing closed in 1932. They are equally popular with collectors today.

For 1904, Greenly redesigned the original Bing free-lance "Black Prince", continuing the popularity of the model. Also from 1904, the clockwork GWR 4–4–0 City of Bath class "Sydney" faithfully recreated the idiosyncratic features of the original, with outside frames for driving and bogie wheels, inside cylinders, coupling rods and springs outside the frames, brass valve cover and copper chimney (see page 62). Another much admired and graceful locomotive was issued in 1913 – the SECR (South East and Chatham Railway) Wainwright "D"; the original was designed by H.S. Wainwright and built in Ashford, Kent, in 1901. It made no concession to modern trends like streamlining, but remained elegant, with curving splashers running neatly into the cab sheets, sparkling brasswork and smart livery.

The 1911 model of Ivatt's famous 4–4–2 GNR Atlantic was also finely modelled, with the parabolic Wootton firebox that was to become such a distinctive feature of the "Flying Scotsman" (see page 102). Although the locomotive body and tender are well designed, the model was let down by the under-scale wheels, with ungainly thick tyres. A less glamorous but no less engaging model was introduced in 1913 in Gauge I and II – Ivatt's compact GNR (Great Northern Railway) N1 0–6–2 condensing tank locomotive, designed for working the steep North London suburban gradients. Its kinship to Gresley's N2 of 1920–21 (see page 145) is apparent. For some reason, many of these locomotives are also often found in nearly new condition.

Bassett-Lowke's LNWR "Precursor" 4–4–2 Tank Locomotives are common in 0 Gauge and Gauge I. Early soldered and hand-painted models of the improved George the Fifth class are scarcer, such as the 4–4–0 "Queen Mary", in 0 Gauge only, and the "George the Fifth" itself, also available in Gauge I and Gauge II. The common tabbed and lithographed version was introduced in 1913.

In 1914 Bassett-Lowke issued a Caledonian Railway 4–4–0 "Dunalastair" No. 142 and eight-wheel tender in the distinctive Scottish blue livery. In the same year Bing also produced for Bassett-Lowke one of its finest pre-war models after a handsome prototype: the Gauge I Great Central Railway 4–6–0 "Sir Sam Fay", named after the railway's general manager. With long, straight splashers over the driving wheels – similar to Drummond's LSWR T14 "Paddlebox" – it has a distinctive form, well expressed in the model. Although sought after, it is relatively common, being listed in the catalogue from 1914 to 1935.

below: Bing's George III "Black Prince" in Midland Railway livery from 1904. The painted boiler, engraved connecting rods and cast axle box indicate that this is a deluxe example.

A fine Carette Great Northern locomotive appeared in the 1911 catalogue, as a Continental version of the Ivatt Atlantic that Carette had supplied to Bassett-Lowke since 1907. Despite the plain livery, it has some of the elegance of the original, with its parabolic firebox and boxy cab.

A further disguised model was the Carette live-steam 4–4–0 Gauge I locomotive in Continental livery, but better known as the 513/48 North Eastern Railway "Smith Compound". Available in Gauge III, it is a high-quality sturdy and heavy toy, using many cast iron parts, including the splashers, cab sides and footplate. With its great curved splashers and cylinders it was an elegant piece, if far too heavy.

At the cheaper end of the ranges made for Bassett-Lowke in the early days, the mainstay was Carette's "storkleg" locomotives. Allied to these, but much more appealing, was the live-steam 2–2–2 "Lady of the Lake",

which appeared in 1903. She carried a much more elaborate hand-painted body, with her name in gold on the single graceful curved splasher. Although the mechanism was similar to the "storkleg", it was one of the first toy locomotives produced in quantity with a body close to the design of the original. It is very rare: the only example to arrive at Christie's was delivered on the back of an open truck, broken up in trunks full of dismantled locomotive components and scrap metal. Despite having lain under piles of rubbish for half a century and being incomplete, she fetched a large sum.

Other famous locomotives made by Carette for Bassett-Lowke include the GNR "Stirling Single" and the European version of the 4–4–0 Vauclain Compound, with the cowcatcher and bell removed and buffers added.

Märklin had dipped early into the British market. Although most of its 1900–02 catalogue was for the

GREAT WESTERN

left: *Bing's Gauge I GWR "Sydney", which appeared in 1904, was the first attempt to reproduce a particular locomotive as a model – a success despite the awkward proportions.*

German market, it presented a small range of 0–4–0 locomotives and coaches in Great Northern Railway (GNR) and London and North Western Railway (LNWR) liveries, and No. C1021 and D1021 4–4–0s for both companies. They were mechanically identical, with only minor livery variations. The accompanying LNWR coaches were the same as the No. 1841 bogie type used for the Schnellbahn and the Serpolletwagen. Of exceptional rarity is the large Central Station (No. 2144) with adjacent "Bagage Room" (sic), one of the earliest English-lettered pieces, dating from 1900–02.

New locomotives in popular outlines came available in 1903. The first was the 2–4–0 "Charles Dickens". The high-voltage electric version had heavy plated motor frames designed to look like coupling rods to support the end of the wheel bearings. Another was the GNR live-steam E4021 with six-wheel tender (see page 64).

Until the introduction of a six-coupled mechanism in 1909, Märklin made use of electric and clockwork four-coupled mechanisms in a host of variations and gauges for different companies or countries. A humble example from the 1904 catalogue is a little Gauge I No. B1021 Locomotive and Tender in LNWR or Midland Railway (MR) livery. Similarly, there is a little 15.5cm (6in) No. 1844 bogie Passenger Post and Luggage Van, which very occasionally appears in Great Eastern Railway livery.

On a grander scale, a very rare Gauge III live-steam LNWR 4–4–0 locomotive and tender appeared in the 1904 catalogue. It is based on the earlier German version, but with a different cab, chimney, splashers, boiler front and tender. The LNWR No. 1841 bogie coach was on an equally massive scale and is also very rare.

Sales of such grand pieces as these were necessarily limited, and after 1910 Gamages department store, which marketed Märklin, only imported pieces in Gauge I and 0 Gauge.

Only two years later, Märklin produced a more accurate model of a distinguished French import: in a brief break from home-grown production, the Great Western Railway ordered a de Glehn Compound 4–4–2 Atlantic "La France" (see page 26). Märklin gave her the correct running number, 102, and their own number, CE1021. Also in 1906, Märklin introduced the E1021 MR 4–4–0, with the running number 2709. It was finished in Midland Railway's lake livery, and came with the rare 1899 MR Bogie Coach and 1900 MR Dining Car.

below: Märklin's Gauge I British-market Great Northern steam locomotive was made in 1904 for sale through Gamages, the London department store.

One of the most unusual prototypes for a Märklin van was a GNR Racehorse Box, which was issued in 1909 as No. 2865. The model had two large roof ventilators and special doors, with the bottom half dropping down as a ramp down which the horses could be led and a pair of side-hinged doors above.

In 1911, Märklin modelled a rare failure from GWR. "The Great Bear" was GWR's only 4–6–2 Pacific locomotive, built in 1908, and was no beauty, either in real life or as a toy (see opposite). To its chagrin, GWR found that the locomotive was too long to negotiate the curved track section into her London terminus, Paddington Station, without hitting the platform edge. Although it made good use of the new six-coupled mechanism, the toy could not be described as beautiful. It remained in Märklin's catalogue until 1923, which means that its value is relatively low compared to others of the period. In the same year Märklin's London and South Western Railway 4–6–0 "Paddlebox" locomotive and tender also used the six-coupled mechanism – "paddlebox" because of the shape of its splashers. It shared the same rather ugly tender as "The Great Bear" and is scarce today, with fewer than six known to exist.

Märklin also supplied accessories to Britain, but they were not specially designed for the British market, so were not popular; consequently they are now rare.

MÄRKLIN AND THE US MARKET

By 1900, the USA was clearly on its way to becoming the most powerful economic and political force in the new world of the twentieth century. However, its material needs were still supplied from the Old World, with a large proportion of toys sold in the USA before 1914 coming from Germany. Because of the vast size of the country and the number of remote rural settlements, very rare and early Märklin pieces are still turning up as "barn finds".

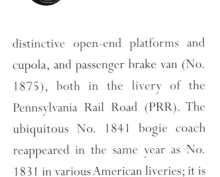

The earliest American-market train appeared in 1898, and was still available in Märklin's 1900–02 catalogue. It was known as the "Eagle", after the transfers on the coach sides. The simple No. 1031 4–4–0 clockwork locomotive was a special design, not an adapted German version; it was decorated with the usual American features of large cab and chimney, bell and cowcatcher. The passenger cars were plain but pleasing, with special open-end platforms and early pattern bogies. The whole set is now very scarce and much sought after, as only four or five are known to survive.

The 1904 catalogue brought a wider range of stock, including the No. AE4021 live-steam 4–4–0 locomotive with cars, including a caboose (No. 1935), with its distinctive open-end platforms and cupola, and passenger brake van (No. 1875), both in the livery of the Pennsylvania Rail Road (PRR). The ubiquitous No. 1841 bogie coach reappeared in the same year as No. 1831 in various American liveries; it is very sought after as the famous "Twentieth Century Limited" that the New York Central ran to Chicago or as the "Royal Blue Limited". Freight cars included a cattle truck (No. 1871) and PRR horsebox (No. 1872).

The first really accurate and model-like bogie freight cars appeared in 1907, such as the San Diego and Arizona Railway Oil Tank Car (No. 2826), NYC Hopper Coal

top: *Looking for uses for its six-coupled mechanism, Märklin produced the ill-fated GWR "Great Bear" in 1911.*

above: *The 1898 Märklin 4–4–0 for the American market, the firm's first large locomotive.*

above: *The Märklin Gauge I Sea Fish Wagon is usually in German, so this Dutch version from 1909 is very rare.*

Truck (No. 2929) and gondola or open wagon (No. 2930). Märklin also introduced the first two in a range of their most popular decorative American freight cars, with colourful beer advertising on the sides: No. 1884P "Pabst Blue Ribbon" and No. 1884S S "Schlitz". Further cars in the series came out in 1913, such as No. 2935 "Heinz Ketchup" and No. 2960 "Budweiser". Early examples were hand painted; later ones were lithographed. The similar No. 2926 NYC Box Car looked plain by comparison.

The finest of all sets of the period was hauled by a magnificent clockwork No. AH1021 PRR Pacific locomotive and tender and followed by the new bogie Pullman cars: Sleeping Car, Parlor Car, Smoking and Baggage Car and Observation Car. All were fitted with elaborate and detailed American-style interiors, belying their plain exteriors. The train looks absolutely perfect when standing at the rare No. 2913 Newark Station, shown only in the 1913 catalogue.

THE FRENCH MARKET

France was also an important export market, but the Märklin catalogue offered French buyers less variety than in other markets.

In 1907 Märklin produced its earliest and finest French market steam locomotive: the No. E1022 Paris Lyon Méditerranée (PLM) Coupe-Vent 4–4–0 (2–2–0). It was modelled on the modern "Grande C" compound locomotive of 1898 that hauled the wealthy to the Côte d'Azur. As its name "Coupe-Vent" (wind-cutter) suggests, it had advanced streamlining for its day. Märklin caught the lines of the original body well, although both the driving wheels and the tender look shrivelled by comparison with the prototype.

Märklin's next PLM locomotive, the No. 1020 of 1912, was of more conventional Pacific outline, with a streamlined cab front. As with many post-1909 models, it was more accurate, with the wheels and bogie tender closer to scale.

The most common type of Märklin French-market locomotives were models of the Paris–Orléans E1 "Steeplecab" electric locomotives, of which there were various 0 Gauge and Gauge I models still in production in the 1930s. The first versions, from 1908, are relatively scarce – No. CL3021 was essentially a Central London Railway locomotive painted dark green, with handrails attached to the bonnets and a dummy pantograph fitted to the roof.

Unusually, Bing also produced an E1 (No. 180/541) for the French market in 1910, but the very plain grey finish with red lining was a long way from the exuberance of earlier pieces.

In 1909, Märklin introduced three new vehicles: two Postes et Telegraphes vans finished in warm brown – No. 2990 four-wheel and No. 2992 bogie – and a double-decker coach with open-sided upper seating deck (No. 2991), as used in the Paris suburbs. The coach is extremely rare, and prone to being faked – since the original manufacture involved altering an existing No. 1866 coach, unscrupulous people have since sold replicas by using new roofs.

Relettering was a simpler way of producing export models. No. 1849 "Seefisch–Nordenham" reappeared in Dutch as "Zeevish–Ymuiden" and the rare No. 2993 prison van reappeared as "Ministère de l'Intérieur, Administration Pénitentiaire" (see page 46). The covered platform from the British No. 2849 station became a Paris Métro platform, No. 2842 Arnstadt Station transformed into Nogent and the rare No. 02018 Central-Bahnhof became Gare-Centrale.

Bowing to the rising tide of nationalism, the French style "& Cie" was used for the company name on these exports, and the 1911 French catalogue made no mention of the German origin of the firm. Indeed, the nameboard above the proudly illustrated factory has had "Metall Spielwären Fabrik" and "Göppingen" scratched out of the artwork.

below: *The French PLM Pacific was Märklin's most popular locomotive using the six-coupled mechanism. Introduced before World War I, production of the model continued throughout the 1920s.*

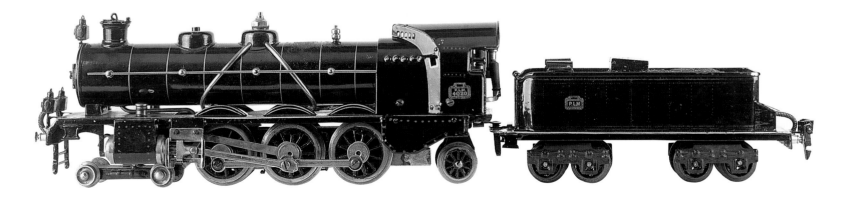

chapter 3

1919–1939

MÄRKLIN, GOING FROM RECOVERY TO STRENGTH

There is no doubt that many politicians at the Treaty of Versailles in 1919 believed that they had created a peace to ensure that "the war to end all wars" was indeed just that. Britain's prime minister, the wily Lloyd George, thought otherwise. He believed that trouble would lie in store if Germany received harsh financial and political punishment. As early as 1921, Germany fell behind with war reparations and entered a disastrous period of hyper-inflation; by November 1923 the mark was worth 30 million times less against sterling and the US dollar than it had been in January of the same year. Financial disaster hurt the middle classes cruelly, exacerbating the political instability of the next sixteen years.

In the midst of this financial meltdown, the toy-train industry was trying to survive. Georges Carette had left Germany at the outbreak of World War I and by the 1930s other firms that had been the backbone of the German toy

below: The Gauge I Leipzig Station's main hall could be expanded, by the addition of extra walls, sheds and platforms, into a truly giant complex.

industry were failing. The once mighty firm of Ernst Plank was fading out by the mid 1930s when it was taken over by Fleischmann. Bing was also badly affected by the Depression: its cheaper range allowed a smaller profit margin than its principal rival, Märklin, and although Britain continued to be a major market, its exports dwindled. The company struggled on through the 1920s, and it did have several successes, including its tabletop railway (see page 99), but, although it was still producing good-quality 0 Gauge models, the company went into receivership on 24 August 1932. Much of the European toy industry at this time was run by Jewish manufacturers and wholesalers, the Bing family included, so the accession of Adolf Hitler to absolute power in March 1933 was a further blow to the industry.

Not all firms went under. Karl Bub of Nürnberg survived by making inexpensive lithographed toy train sets, usually with simple clockwork or electric B (0–4–0) locomotives and lightweight coaches. Bub also took over some of Carette's, and later Bing's, old toy-train tooling.

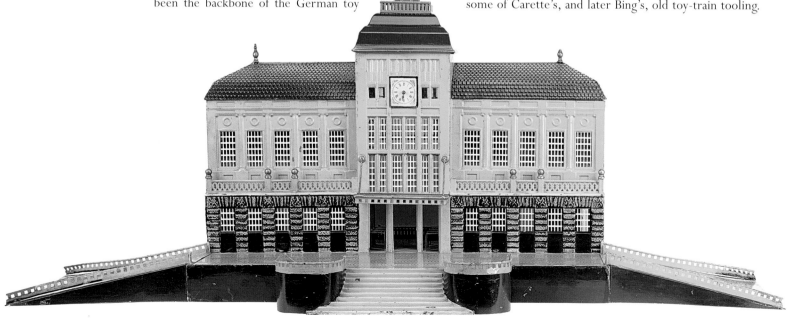

Kraus-Fandor, which had begun as the firm of Joseph Kraus in Nürnberg before World War I, produced a range of inexpensive and rather flimsy electric and clockwork trains that are still of small value today. It partly financed Dorfan in the USA (from which came the reversed name – Fandor – for home use), and could still produce commendable pieces.

Despite the vicissitudes of the Depression, a depleted workforce and a perpetual shortage of materials, Märklin survived the early post-war years. It did not suffer as badly as some other companies because it had always maintained good domestic sales of high-margin products. Its range through the 1920s was not as adventurous as before 1914, but it still sold enough elaborate and expensive toys to maintain its position as the pre-eminent German toy-train manufacturer. Märklin pioneered and maintained the finest standards of production, supported by brand awareness, and remained as market leader through war and economic catastrophe. It still thrives today as the only major model train company still manufacturing in Europe.

MÄRKLIN PRODUCTION RESTARTS

The output of the Märklin factory had been concentrated on war work, so their 1915 catalogue offered only a limited range, concentrating heavily on guns, limbers and other military vehicles. The railway theme was limited to ambulance and gun and limber wagons in 0 Gauge and Gauge I, a very rare clockwork miniature ambulance in the Lilliput series and armoured trains. They were identified as 00 Gauge, but the rail gauge was 26mm (1¹/₁₆in) rather than the 16.5mm (¹¹/₁₆in) gauge used later by Märklin, Trix and Hornby-Dublo.

above: *The popular Märklin tram set appeared during the 1920s in a variety of different colour schemes.*

It took several years to rebuild the workforce; many craftsmen had perished or gone into other businesses and it took time to rebuild old skills. In the meantime, a large range was offered, but with few new items – much of the content of the first post-war catalogue, produced in 1919, was unsold pre-war stock.

An exception was a magnificent new station, known in its most complete form as the 2037GB Großstadt-Bahnhof, but popularly known as Leipzig Station. It may

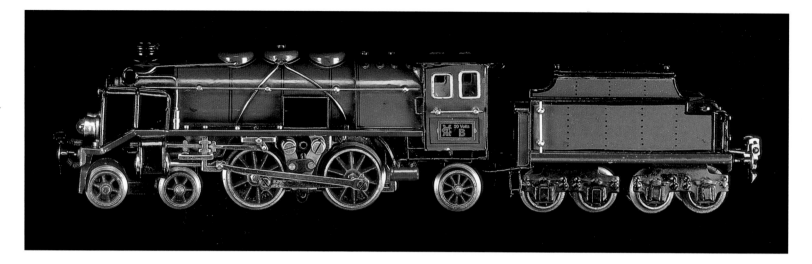

above: *By the end of the 1920s Märklin was concentrating on Deutsche Reichsbahn, the German state railway. This 0 Gauge Atlantic is a typical example.*

well have been designed before the war, but was modern and innovative in several ways. It was more realistic than any toy station produced to date, designed in a restrained Classical manner, closely based on elements of the actual building, which is still the largest station in Europe. The substantial Märklin structure (see page 70) is based around a five-bay module, with large multi-paned windows divided by applied pilasters. This modular pressing was used ingeniously to make the upper front and side elevations of the Gauge I version, flanking a colossal tower, and the complete elevations of the smaller Gauge 0 version that lacked the *piano nobile*.

The main building came with two ramps and a grand flight of steps, leading to a ticket hall that was large enough to produce an echo. On to this could be added further components: two short stub walls surmounted by dummy lanterns, two covered platforms with three separate awnings to cover the running lines and a large flank wall section, built around the same modular pressing.

Early examples, prior to 1925, were fitted inside with oil lamps and transfer tiling on the roof; later examples were unlit and had embossed tiling detail. Using all the different parts, a station could therefore be made as large as funds allowed, and examples today are often the centrepiece of fine collections.

As if to prove that not all 1920s production was handsome, however, in 1925 Märklin introduced the second version of a modern station, 2032, of consummate plainness. It typified the simplicity of the post-war range, by comparison with the Golden Age prior to 1914.

As the 1920s progressed, the range became plainer and more realistic, with less hand painting and less handmade work. The range of cheap sets increased in size to accommodate the weaker market, and developments continued with the introduction of the clockwork or electric 3070/72 two-unit tramcar in 1925 (see page 71).

The first "new generation" large locomotive that set the tone for the fine creations of the 1930s was the 1928 CER65/13020, an Atlantic (2' B 1'). It looked more modern and realistic than any other locomotive issued to date and was finished in a stylish dark grey livery (see opposite). The locomotive hauled an eight-wheel (bogie) tender with neatly scalloped platework at both ends of the coal deck, a feature that was to be carried over to the slightly longer tender that accompanied the HR64/13020 Pacific (2' C 1') the following year. The HR series provided the most popular heavy traction in the Märklin range during the 1930s.

To accompany the Gauge I versions of these locomotives, in 1929 Märklin also introduced 53cm (20in) bogie coaches in the liveries of Mitropa, Deutsche Reichsbahn and Compagnie Internationale des Wagons-Lits. Despite their size, they were still not scale length by comparison with the prototypes, but they certainly did form eye-catching rakes.

In 1927 Märklin introduced a fine 20-volt electric three-car model representing the Köln–Bonner Rheinüferbahn tram (RHU64/13021/35/3). It was solidly produced in Gauge I only and hand painted in cream with tan roof (see below); it is difficult to find in good condition today.

Freight stock also became more realistic at this time, with a new range of open wagons and vans, beer and tank wagons. Mostly, these freight wagons are cheaper to buy today, but there are exceptions, such as the 1975G Tunnel Repair Wagon from 1926, which is very hard to find.

below: *The imposing Rheinüferbahn from 1927 was only made in Gauge I and in three-car sets. This was Märklin's last attempt to produce an electric inter-urban set and it was never catalogued.*

DEVELOPMENTS IN THE EXPORT MARKET

France was honoured in 1919 by receiving some of Märklin's first new post-war models, the V3021 B and CL64/3021 Bo-Bo, which updated the PO E1 "steeple-cab" electric locomotives derived from the old Central London Railway. The B

(four-wheel) locomotive was a good model, but very common in its various stages of development, so not expensive today.

The reverse is true of the 53cm (20in) 1945G bogie coaches designed in 1920 to accompany the revived pre-war H64/3021 PLM Pacific, representing the train taking the new generation of the European wealthy to the South of France. Painted in black, with red, yellow or green upper parts over black to represent first, second and third classes, the G suffix means that they were fitted with detailed interiors. Together they look very fine, particularly with the 1946G Teak Restaurant Car and the 1947G Blue Sleeping Car.

below: The biggest locomotive Märklin made for the British market was the "Flying Scotsman". Most were steamers, but a few Gauge I electric version have been found.

For the British market, Märklin carried over several smaller models from before the war, including the CE4021 North British Railway "Atlantic", which is surprisingly common in its electric variant, but rarer in live-steam in good condition; it was looking rather long in the tooth by the time of its withdrawal in 1928. On the other hand, Great Northern Railway locomotives such as the E1031 in 1923 and the 1929 CE1021 GNR Ivatt "Atlantic" still looked distinguished in their last years.

In the late 1920s, W. Seelig, Märklin's British agent, issued the Better Toys range of very detailed English-language pamphlet catalogues, with editorial copy from a distinguished British enthusiast, helping to make the German origins of the range seem remote. A wide range of four- and six-coupled tank and tender locomotives was produced through the 1920s in various liveries; they all have their merits, but some larger models stand out. The most notable was a live-steam model of the most famous British locomotive, the "Flying Scotsman", which was produced from 1925 to 1929. Sadly, it was not one of their most accurate models: the fluid lines of the parabolic Wootton firebox remained resolutely cylindrical, with a couple of "wings" tacked on each side, although the splashers, footplate and cab are well handled, and in

Gauge I it did embody the massive elegance of the original (see opposite). The chances of finding the similar Southern Railway "Lord Nelson" in any shape or form are even slimmer. Märklin produced it between 1925 and 1927, but only a few are known to exist today, and their lack of accuracy does not make them any less appealing to collectors.

In 1923, Märklin reintroduced several versions of the TCE 1021 tank locomotive in different pre-grouping liveries, all using four-coupled mechanisms. The most common represented the 4–4–2 LNWR "Precursor" — remarkably similar to the version Bing made for Bassett-Lowke — in black livery. A very similar locomotive also appeared in Marsh brown LBSCR livery. The smartest version of all was the 2–4–4 MR "Flat Iron" in lake livery, which had distinctively long bunkers and side tanks with openings in front of the driving wheels fitted with steps and hand-irons (see above).

Also in 1923 there appeared a revised range of locomotives using six-coupled mechanisms. The smaller 0–6–0 tank locomotives make good workhorses, but the larger tank locomotives, such as the TH 1021 LNWR "Bowen-Cooke" 4–6–2, look like an oversized "Precursor", but are far less common. Probably the most popular with collectors of the British-outline tank locomotive is the Baltic 4–6–4 TK 1021; this is occasionally found in other liveries, but is best known as the Southern Railway "Stephenson", with the name of the great locomotive designers and engineers emblazoned on the tank sides. Because Robert Stephenson & Co. actually built the first locomotive to run in Germany (see page 87), German collectors have a particular penchant for this model.

above: *The Midland "Flat Iron" tank engine was a creditable attempt at a scale model and was made by Märklin for Gamages in the 1920s.*

Märklin's coaching stock for the British market closely followed the work that Bing was carrying out for Bassett-Lowke at the same time. Simple lithographed four-wheel coaches were available in the liveries of the Big Four rail companies, but bogie coaches only appeared in LMS lake or LNER teak. As revising lithography was an expensive process, the MR inscriptions of the old coaches were painted out and re-lettered LMS, and sometimes window frames were hand painted as the die stamps for pressing out the openings tended to remove the lithographic ink. The most sought-after British coach is the hand-painted 2890 bogie Pullman, which is beautifully detailed in cream and brown livery, and has blue-shaded detail representing glass in the small window lights and oval lavatory windows.

below: *Märklin's Be 4/6 "Gothard" successfully conveyed the locomotive's almost brutal strength and solidity. Weak points are the plain pantographs and the huge headlights.*

The most interesting improvement in Märklin's Swiss range was in electric traction, with the introduction in 1921 of the S64/3021 Bo-Bo "Gothard" (see below). Hand-painted in deep brown, it was a good representation of the new Be 4/6 heavy Swiss locomotives and bristled with three large headlight bulbs; the wheel arrangement had been simplified by dropping the external coupling rods and inclined bar drive of the original. In 1926 it was followed by the simpler RS 3030 four-wheel version and in 1927 by the larger CS65/13021 4–4–2 (2' B 1'), which had protruding bonnets at each end, after the Ae 3/6 locomotive. The most impressive of the group was the 2' C 1' HS65/13020 of 1929, also with dummy pantographs and protruding bonnets.

Two models produced for the American market just after World War I have attained the status of great rarities. The first was the clockwork version of the AVE 1021 2–4–2 (1'B'1) New York Central Tunnel Locomotive, only issued in 1919 (see opposite). The second was an 0–4–0 NYCL Tunnel Locomotive, available only in 1922–3 and in 0 Gauge. It was a hybrid created from the bodies of the AVR 1030 NYCL Tunnel Locomotive and the 2943 PRR Passenger Baggage Van and ran mounted on an oval monorail track. Today, only a few are known to exist.

In 1929 Märklin introduced a further use for the 2890 British Pullman body, using it to make up a 20-volt three-car Electric Multiple Unit in green and yellow for the Dutch market (NL 13020/3). Despite

its completely fanciful appearance, it has great appeal. Two years later, Märklin found a final use for the 2890 British Pullman – this time as the three-car MOB "Golden Mountain" Pullman (see page 78), which was finished in a beautiful blue and cream finish and is almost impossible to find as a complete unit.

THE "SUPERMODELL" ERA

The early to mid-1930s represented a second Golden Age for Märklin, but in a very different way from the early years of the twentieth century. Production was getting closer to model-like accuracy, lacking the bright and nursery-friendly qualities of the older toys. Of course, the resulting trains were superbly built, with a great diversity of locomotives, stock and accessories available. Märklin's

effortless but rather clinical superiority was a reflection in microcosm of the rapidly growing industrial and economic might of Germany, boosted by injections of government money. With the demise of Bing and the addition of Karl Bub's range to its own in 1933, Märklin was left with little serious domestic competition.

This period is known as the "Supermodell" era, as increasingly powerful-looking models of locomotives from around the world appeared. Catalogues were now printed for the benefit of customers rather than retailers, with pieces well illustrated in colour with descriptive text and clear pricing. Production of 0 Gauge became increasingly important as Gauge I started to fade out, making its last appearance in

above: *The extremely rare hand-painted Märklin Bo-Bo NYC S3 AVE1021, from 1919, was only available in clockwork.*

catalogue D-14 for 1937–8. The contents of this catalogue represented the zenith of the pre-war range.

The 4–4–0 E66 Tender Locomotive appeared in 1931. It was painted in Deutsche Reichsbahn black livery, as was the 4–6–0 GR66 Tender Locomotive, which appeared in 1933; together they were the "workhorses" of a typical layout of reasonable size. In 1935 they both received the "70" motor with revised remote reverse mechanism.

An eccentric addition appeared in 1931 – the SZ12970 model of the Zeppelin Railcar. Designed by Franz Kruckenberg, it had a streamlined nose and cockpit like a modern aircraft, silver body and large driving propeller at the rear; apart from shedding two pairs of driving wheels, it was a good representation of the original.

below: The status of this Märklin "Golden Mountain" Pullman coach is reflected in its hand-painted finish and exceptional rarity.

Also influenced by Zeppelin technology, Wumag of Görlitz developed the VT877a/b, a high-speed two-unit railcar to run between Berlin and Hamburg, known as the "Flying Hamburger". It was powered by two Maybach 410hp engines with electric transmission and could reach 160kmh (100mph), with 102 passengers looked after in style by a crew from the luxurious Mitropa service. The Märklin TW12970 model is very faithful to the original, capturing well the experimental streamlined appearance and the bright violet and cream colour scheme. It is most commonly found in the post-1934 version in cream and red livery.

In 1932 the revised version of the HR Pacific was introduced in black or green livery, more closely following the design of the original and celebrated DR "01" locomotive. The model had now acquired the correct 4–4–T32 tender and Heusinger valve gear, with other details such as large Wagner-pattern smoke deflectors following in 1938. It was a mainstay of the range throughout the 1930s and a powerful-looking model, particularly in the form of the huge live-steam HR4921 (see page 80), which was only available in its final form for three years and was extremely costly even before the war.

That year, 1932, brought a design development that would have completely changed the market – had it not remained only at prototype stage. The proposed S Gauge was smaller than 0 Gauge, but it enabled coaches to be produced to scale length and still fit a layout of average size. Sadly, the range of locomotive, freight stock and

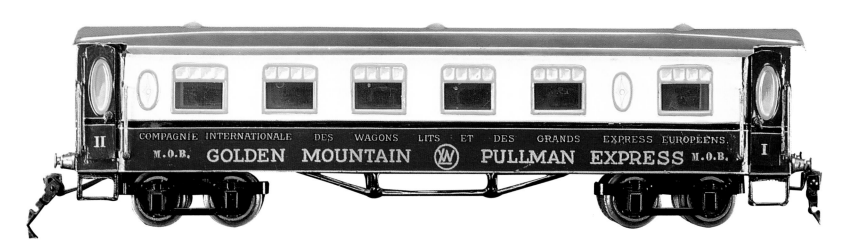

coaches never made it on to the market, and can only be seen as hand-built models in the Märklin Museum in Göppingen (see above).

It was in 1932 that the first export-market "Supermodell" appeared. This was the AHR66/13020 New York Central 4–6–4 Hudson Locomotive and Tender; in its earliest and rarest form it had a silver-painted smokebox, which was later painted black (see page 81). But it was the second "Supermodell" that was probably the most famous locomotive ever built by Märklin: the "Krokodil".

After the chaos of poor coal supplies in Switzerland during World War I, the Schweizerische Bundesbahn (SBB) invested in electrification and needed a new articulated heavy-freight locomotive that was able to cope with steep gradients and sharp curves. The Ce 6/8 – popularly known as the "Krokodil" after its long, green and slightly menacing outline – was the result, built in Wintherthur by Schweizerische Lokomotiv- und Maschinenfabrik (SLM). Thirty-three of the best known Ce 6/8 II type were made between 1920 and 1921; a further eighteen

were produced up to 1927. They had a 1'C C 1' wheel arrangement, with two large engines under the long bonnets at each end developing around 3,000hp. Power was transmitted to the leading driving wheels by inclined bar drive, in which a carrier axle drove a weighty angled beam that was in turn connected by a conventional coupling rod to the centre and trailing wheels.

Märklin's versions, the 20-volt CCS66/12920 in 0 Gauge and the 12921 in Gauge I, were introduced in 1933 (see page 81). These magnificent creatures brilliantly caught the lines of the real locomotive and were as powerful as they looked. The smaller model was briefly available with one motor, but otherwise both were equipped with the more desirable twin motors up to the end of production in 1940. The carrier axle flywheel is a distinctive feature of the models, but the complex drive system of the prototype has been replaced by a single coupling rod. Also, the six driving wheels at each end of the full-size locomotive have been replaced by four, in order to cope with the tighter curves

above: *Many Märklin products are rare, but these fine 1932 S Gauge prototypes in the Märklin Museum are unique.*

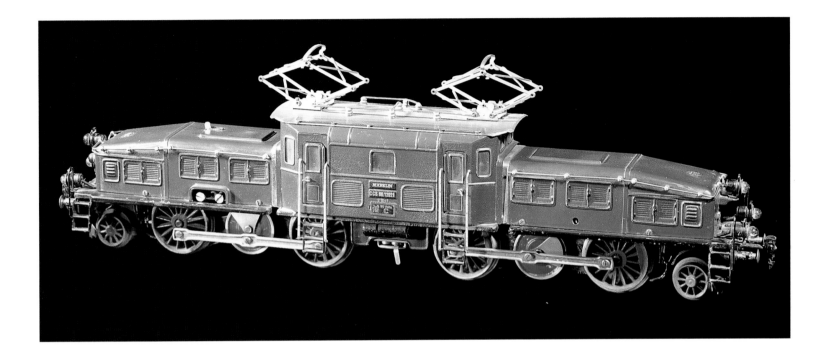

The Märklin "Supermodell" era in the 1930s produced gems for the home and export market. The live-steam plain black and red HR4921 DR Pacific (**top left**) is rarely found in unscorched condition. It towers over the elegant NYC "Hudson" (**left**), but both look small beside the massive Gauge I "Krokodil" Swiss electric locomotive (**above**) – the dream of many collectors.

of toy railway track. At 62.5cm (24½in) long, the Gauge I version was probably the most weighty and substantial toy locomotive in series production.

In 1934 Märklin revised the HS locomotive, with coupling rods now replaced by the tell-tale circular housings for dummy Buchli articulated lever drive. The prototype was devised by Jakob Buchli, a former director of SLM, with each axle independently sprung and driven by a powerful electric motor. Most were built by Brown Boveri & Cie, an antecedent of today's huge Alstom combine. Buchli's design quickly became more popular for express locomotives than the old-fashioned inclined bar drive that was used on the "Krokodil".

below: *For the French market Märklin created the handsome eight-coupled Mountain "Etat" in 1934. Although elegant in grey, the accurate rendering was the alternative black livery.*

In 1934 Märklin also introduced a new eight-coupled mechanism which enabled the production of two of its finest and most handsome models: the French-market 4–8–2 Mountain "Etat" and, in 1935, the British-market LNER 2–8–2 Mikado "Cock o' the North". The French locomotive was well modelled and available in black livery with red detailing. It was also available in a smart grey livery, which can vary in shade from model to model and from one component to another (see below). The Mountain "Etat" never actually ran in such a livery –

Märklin had chosen to copy a locomotive in out-shopped state, just after leaving the works, painted in grey photographic finish.

The "Cock o' the North" was the first of a class of six P2 locomotives designed by the innovative chief mechanical engineer of the London North Eastern Railway (LNER), Sir Nigel Gresley (see page 106). They were built in Doncaster between 1934 and 1936 to haul passenger expresses over the heavy gradients between Edinburgh and Aberdeen. The "Cock o' the North" was his first experiment with streamlining, or air-smoothing as it was also called. She had a semi-streamlined nose, designed to cut wind resistance and deflect smoke from the driver's view. The smokebox had a canted front with double chimney, flanked by smoke deflectors that ran back smoothly into the top of the boiler like bats' wings; this was combined with high splashers and eight driving wheels 188 cm (6ft 2in) in diameter, to give a long engine of unrivalled grace and elegance. Sadly, the entire class was mutilated by Gresley's successor and scrapped many years ago. The "Cock o' the North", in particular, is still so much admired by enthusiasts that a plan is afoot to build a replica from scratch.

Märklin modelled her as L20/12920, in green livery as 2001 and in black freight livery with running number

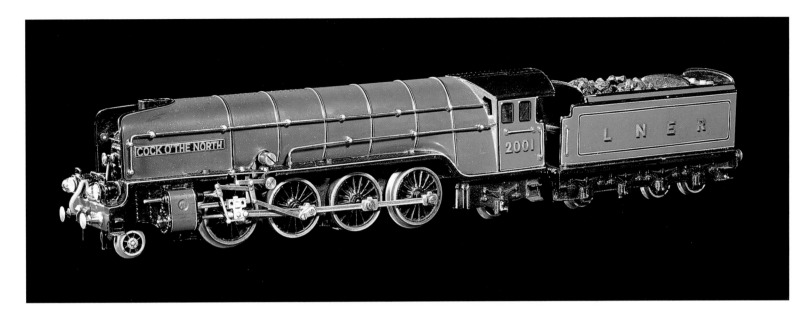

2002 on the nameplates; the lettering on the nameplates can often look rather wobbly (see above), but this is a correct feature. In some ways the model outstrips reality, as the heavy-gauge tinplate makes the real platework look rather flimsy. Very few models were imported into Britain and it is one of the most sought-after pieces from this period, although several modern German makers have satisfied demand by building good-quality replicas.

A new 0 Gauge 2924/2925 Pullman for the American market appeared in 1934; it was scale length at a hefty 53cm (20in) long and was fitted with the only twelve-wheel bogies made by Märklin. It was available in a realistic shade of Pullman green, with body rivets raised in relief, and in such names as "Cromwellian" and "Croton" (see page 84). They were pricey items at the time and are now sufficiently rare that even to see a rake of these coaches would be a dream for most collectors.

At this time Märklin was also making a range of the smaller 0 Gauge coaches, from 11cm (4½in) upwards.

The greatest piece for the domestic market also appeared in 1934: the scale-length bogie coach, 40cm (16in) long in 0 Gauge and 53cm (20in) long in Gauge I. Although it is still undersized compared to the original, it does look very imposing, particularly when fitted with optional interior sleeping, dining or seating detail. The standard dark green 1941 Deutsche Reichsbahn models (see page 87) are quite easily available, complemented by the 1944 Baggage Van. Less often found are versions finished in Mitropa's dark red livery, issued as dining cars (1942), sleeping cars (1943) and baggage vans (1944). Versions in the dark blue livery of the Compagnie Internationale des Wagons-Lits were also issued, using the same reference numbers but with a "J" suffix.

A humbler issue from 1934 was the 2–4–2 TCE66/12920 tank locomotive. Quite popular with collectors, it is far surpassed by its big brother, issued in

above: *Few locomotives can rival the semi-streamlined beauty of Gresley's "Cock o' the North", faithfully captured by Märklin. The six locomotives in the class were all named after Sir Walter Scott characters.*

1935 with improved distant reverse. The TK70/12920 is a chunky and solid 4–6–4, essentially a Pacific with four-wheel rear bogie, coal bunker and enclosed cab added. It is rarely found in good condition and fakes with replica cabs joined to original Pacifics have turned up on the market (see page 86).

An important advance in 1935 was a new range of electric 0 Gauge solid steel rail, with large radius curves. To date, track had been made of light, hollow tinplate, with poor profile and tight curves that would not accommodate the wheelbase of the new large locomotives. The resulting "Modellschienen" was a work of art in its own right, particularly the points, which are much sought after.

The next two introductions took one giant step back and one forward in time. The first was a special 0 Gauge train, "Der Adler", made for German railways, commemorating the centenary of the opening of Bavaria's Ludwigsbahn between Nürnberg and Fürth on 7 December 1835. Given the tense political situation in 1935, it was paradoxical that the locomotive was made by Robert Stephenson & Co. of Newcastle and driven by an Englishman, William Wilson. It was correctly modelled by Märklin as a 1' A 1' (2–2–2), with top-hatted driver and brakeman. In real life the locomotive is as small as it

above: *Large and handsome, just right for the American market: the massive Märklin US Pullman from 1934 was their only twelve-wheel coach. It is very rare today.*

looks in the model, but with a long, slim stovepipe chimney. It came with a rake of coaches, appearing like horsedrawn vehicles on wagon chassis. The less fortunate sat on benches in open trucks and Märklin provided a range of composition figures in period dress, some with tiny parasols (see page 86). The model is exquisite, and rarely suffers from playwear, but is prone to metal fatigue in the wheels, and passengers and chimney have sometimes been replaced.

From the first German steam locomotive, the next introduction was very different: the latest record-breaker from Borsig. In 1935 the famous firm of August Borsig of Berlin introduced the "05" class of three fully streamlined three-cylinder locomotives. On 11 May 1936 the second of the class broke the world speed record at 200.4 kmh (124.5mph), which stood until Sir Nigel Gresley's "Mallard" took it in 1938.

Märklin chose to model the first examples with conventional cab, as SLH70/12920, rather than with the unusual forward control cab of the third example in the class. They captured the rather organic appearance of the prototype well, although its wheel arrangement was simplified from 2' C 2' to 2' C 1' (see opposite). With such a large area of smooth platework, the model is very vulnerable to damage or paint loss and is consequently very sought after in perfect condition.

The last three entirely new 0 Gauge models were introduced some years before World War II. Two of these represented the latest lightweight electric "Triebwagen" or express railcars of Schweizerische Bundesbahn or SBB, the Swiss railway. The first, the RP12930, was the Rbe 2/4 "Roter Pfeil" – Red Arrow – which appeared in 1936. This was a single-unit passenger vehicle with bonnets at each end, finished in bright red livery, making a highly esteemed toy of very modern appearance; the original is still running today and hardly looks out of place. In the following year, a model of SBB's other advanced passenger vehicle appeared: the new three-unit BCLe 8/12, which achieved 180kmh (112mph) in trials. Märklin issued it as TW66/12940/3 in violet and cream and in red livery without pantographs. Finally, in 1939, it appeared in the correct SBB red livery with two pantographs and is now scarce.

One of the last prestige locomotives was introduced in around 1937: the "Commodore Vanderbilt". As AK70/12921, it was almost the last of the original series of Gauge I locomotives made by the company. The very

last was the TK66 Tank Locomotive, which appeared in 1938. Both are almost unknown in this guise, being more often found in the 0 Gauge version (see page 88). The original Hudson 4–6–4 New York Central "Commodore Vanderbilt" was the first American streamlined locomotive and commemorated the famous founder of the railway; it was designed by Carl Kantola and was revealed to the public in December 1934. The Märklin model reflects the extraordinary lines of the original well, with a great nose like an eroded cliff and splashers sweeping in long, fluid curves over the wheels – this time in the correct arrangement, unlike the Borsig 05. Despite the solid appearance of the tinplate sheeting, it is in fact easily damaged, particularly at the bottom of the valance at the front. The silver lettering was applied using a stamp and is vulnerable to wear from fingertips.

The 1936–7 Märklin catalogue gives a good cross-section of the 0 Gauge freight stock available in the "Supermodell" era, with a few pieces still in Gauge I. The

below: *Despite looking rather like a mechanized aubergine or eggplant, the casing of the streamlined 1935 "Borsig" was very effective.*

workhorses of the range, and the least expensive to buy today, were the four-wheel open wagons and goods vans, both lithographed in plain brown to imitate planking. They are often found with a brakeman's hut on one end, which would change a 1765 Open Wagon to a 1771 – although "1765" is still printed on the wagon side.

Some of the more valuable and interesting vehicles are the four-wheel flat or low-sided wagons with special loads, including 1707 with clockwork tinplate field tractor, 1709 with crawler tractor, 1764A with diecast motor car, 1706 with painted tinplate "Märklin" removal van and 1983T, with its "Sarrasani" circus cage.

below: *The grimy workaday reputation of tank locomotives is belied by the large Märklin TK tank from 1935, which is much sought after.*

Bogie wagons are also popular collectors' items. The 1855 "50 Tons" Coal Hopper with operating chutes looks particularly exciting and realistic in a long rake. One of the most ingenious wagons, with good play value, is the 1777 Milk Wagon; it carries three pull-along milk tanks, secured by a lever and rod arrangement. It was only made from 1938 to 1939, so is hard to find in good condition. Potential collectors should be

aware that the flat wagon bases were adapted for each load, so these often now have the wrong piece attached. Sad to say, replica parts have been widely made, and can often be used to deceive. Thus, the bright red tinplate car on the 1766 wagon from 1935 can be a replica.

As ever, the quality of Märklin production could be defined by the range of buildings and accessories available for "dressing up" layouts: each piece was hand painted, with stamped lettering applied, and covered every aspect needed. One of the first of the new station designs of the "Supermodell" era was also the largest, the 2039G Stuttgart Station from 1930 (see page 89). It was available

either as left- or right-hand side or as one complete unit and was a remarkably good representation of the original building, although the tower has been brought forward to fit on the plinth. Other, smaller stations that became available reflected the plainer architecture of the day, such as the 2003B station with goods shed. Buildings of this type are much cheaper now than their more decorative predecessors. On the other hand, the large 2015 Station is at least impressive in its plainness. The same modern idiom was used for the stylish 13729/6 Signal Cabin from 1937, with semi-circular ends in the Odéon style. The humble Station Kiosk, 2619G, is more traditional in appearance (see page 89). The entire accessories range extended to platform barrows, refreshment trolleys, ticket machines, destination indicators, figures, electrically operated yard superintendents, clocks, fuel pumps, telephone kiosks, lineside signs and signals. Because they have often been stored away in boxes almost since they were produced, many are as rich and colourful as when they were new.

MÄRKLIN OO GAUGE

Märklin was faced with new realities in the mid-1930s. The quality of their production had been improving considerably in the "Supermodell" era; they were now producing increasingly fine larger-gauge models for a

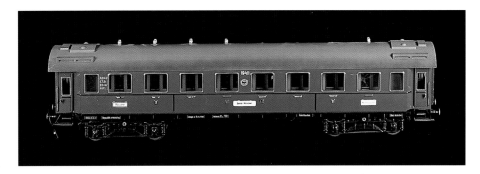

diminishing market. Mindful of the success of the Trix Express miniature electric table railway system that had been launched in March 1935 (see page 110) – and using some of their patents – Märklin launched their own system in the same year. The range grew rapidly, curtailed only by the outbreak of war. With typical attention to detail, Märklin offered buyers not only a range of locomotives, both steam and electric, but also a selection of railcars, rolling stock and, of course, numerous accessories.

Märklin's table-top system was a three-rail 20-volt AC system with 700 hand-operated reverse, and, like their counterparts at Trix and Hornby, the designers took the opportunity to modernize the basic construction of

top: *The centenary Märklin "Der Adler" from 1935 looks out of place in the streamlined era; the British-market model was unnamed.*

above: *Märklin's 40cm (16in) coaches are the finest and most accurate 0 Gauge passenger stock the company produced.*

their new 00 Gauge models. Important parts of the chassis and bodies of the locomotives and coach bogies were now made of *Gußmetall,* or mazac, an alloy based on magnesium and zinc. Mazac was economical and produced excellent castings, but it was also extremely susceptible to what is expressively called in German *Zinkpest* – metal fatigue (see page 128).

below: *In 1937 Märklin captured well the lines of Kantola's extraordinary "Commodore Vanderbilt", with the arc of its high-steppng flanks and nose like an inverted ship's bow.*

Both the B (0–4–0) locomotives introduced with the new system in 1935 were neat designs. The steam R700 had a tinplate boiler with embossed dummy steam pipes leading up to the steam dome, tinplate cab and mazac chassis, splashers and smoke deflectors; it was finished in Deutsche Reichsbahn black livery. Like all the steam locomotives, it had a rather oversized bulb in the middle of the smokebox door and, like them all, suffers from metal fatigue.

The body of the RS700 electric locomotive was entirely made of lithographed tinplate, of Swiss outline with a bonnet at each end, like a miniature 0 Gauge RS66 locomotive. Although it was a good load hauler, the RS700's hand reverse limited its flexibility.

The SLR700, brought out in 1936, was a miniature and anonymous version of the NYC "Commodore Vanderbilt", pictured below. A model of the big DR 01 Pacific, the HR700, that followed in 1937, had the first six-coupled mechanism. This was also used in the HS700 1'B'1 electric locomotive in the same year.

The introduction of the 800 mechanism in 1938 brought great changes, since it provided a "perfect reverse" that could be operated remotely. All the current locomotives were adapted to fit the new mechanism, the most noticeable difference being that the brush caps were now set further back.

A spectacular new locomotive came out in 1939 – the 00 Gauge version of the DR BR06 "Borsig" streamlined record breaker, the dark green SK800. The "Borsig" (see page 85) was such a popular model that it went

through no less than twenty different versions before it was finally withdrawn from the catalogue in 1959. The scarcer green version is the more valuable, and it is rare to find it in good condition: if the locomotive body has not been damaged by metal fatigue, then the tender has usually suffered.

Shaped rather like a miniature "Flying Hamburger" (see page 78), the lithographed tinplate TWE700R was issued in 1936, once again clothing the early hand-reverse mechanism, and with the lever protruding through the roof. The most common version in red and cream is smart enough (see page 90), but other finishes, such as blue, can be worth twice as much, and the extremely rare two-car TW800, which was issued in 1939, is usually worth half as much again. They were only in production for a short time, so not many were manufactured, and as the bodies were made of mazac, they suffered badly from metal fatigue, further increasing their rarity.

While typical interwar rolling stock is bright and appealing, it is not particularly rare because it is made entirely of painted and lithographed tinplate, which survives well. The 342 and 343 Mitropa coaches are collectible, but by comparison the 352 coaches are much scarcer in fine original condition, as the bogie frames and ventilators were made of mazac.

Märklin was acutely aware of the export potential of the 00 Gauge range, however unlikely the outline of the piece. The 342J Wagon-Lits Dining Car for the French market (see page 91) was simply an improved paint finish on the basic 342 coach, but it proved very popular. Although the SLR 700 and 800 mimicked the NYC "Commodore Vanderbilt", Märklin's HR700A was simply a German Pacific with a cowcatcher on the front – nothing special, perhaps, but these Americanized versions are now very scarce.

The most collectible group of locomotives in the entire 00 Gauge range were those originally destined, in 1937 and 1938, for the British market. With just one exception, they were all German or pseudo-American in

left: *Märklin accessories were the icing on the cake. Here it looks as if the news vendor in 1927 has just stepped out for a coffee – or a schnapps.*

below: *The Märklin model of Stuttgart Station from 1930 is uncannily accurate, although compressed to fit on the plinths.*

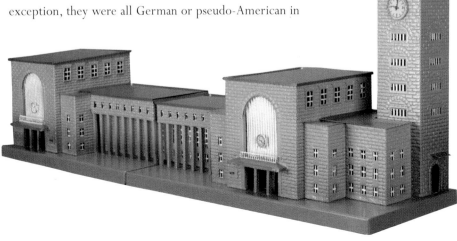

below: *This little streamlined lithographed Märklin TWE 700R 1936 railcar is rare enough, but is surpassed by the very scarce hand-painted 1945 version.*

left: *Based on the standard green DR bogie coach, the blue and gilt Wagon-Lits livery, which dates from 1935, looks more elegant.*

above: *Although it is just a German-outline R700 painted in LMS lake livery, this locomotive from 1937 is still very scarce.*

left: *Tiny, but one of the great Märklin rarities, the E800 was manufactured only in 1938. The body was hand made in tinplate and brass rather than cast in mazac. The rich LMS livery is prone to fading.*

outline, painted and lettered in LMS (London Midland and Scottish) or LNER (London North Eastern Railway) livery. The LMS R700 and LNER HR700 are typically worth between two and four times as much as the German-market version. The rarest model of all appeared in 1938 and sold in tiny numbers (although there is conclusive evidence that some were sold after World War II). It was called the LMS E800 (see pages 90–91) and may look like a fairly undistinguished 4–4–0 Compound, but a good example today would cost as much as a new executive car. The reason lies under the lake livery: the bodies of the locomotive and tender were hand-fabricated from tinplate with brass cylinder chests, not made from injection-moulded mazac or simple pressings like other Märklin 00 Gauge locomotives.

The rare 349 Pullman Coach provided the basis for the even rarer 349EB LNER Pullman, pictured above. The slightly more common 342E LMS Coach (shown opposite) was based on the standard 342 tinplate bogie Dining Car. Much the rarest of all these British-market variations is the 352E LMS Dining Car, based on a more realistic longer vehicle, but prone to suffering from metal fatigue in the bogies and ventilators.

TRAIN SETS

While 00 Gauge passenger and freight sets are now instructive in showing a cross-section of the range, to Märklin at the time they were an excellent way of bringing in customers by supplying them with all the stock they needed at a sensible price. For example, in 1937 the SLR741 Passenger Set could be had for less than a third the cost of the 0 Gauge LNER "Cock o' the North" on its own. And for the price of the HS744 Passenger Set, with its six-coupled mechanism, you could buy instead the huge double-tier SLR 742G set, which packed in a complete layout. That same set today, in pristine condition, would now fetch more than an equally well-preserved "Cock o' the North", even though the lone locomotive originally cost twice as much.

The large SLR742G set is a good example of the type of finely painted and detailed pieces that Märklin sold for dressing up their layouts. A much larger item was shared with the 0 Gauge range – the magnificent 2039G Stuttgart Station. Even rarer is the 453 Tunnel, which is made out of humble wood and painted plaster, with a little tinplate keep; it is large and fragile and understandably is not usually found in good condition. The rarest of all pre-war accessories, however, is a two-bay semi-detached house from the 700/210 retailer's display layout; despite appearances – this small and humble building looks as if it has escaped from a London suburb – it is actually very valuable.

ORIGINALS AND REPLICAS

Today it is almost impossible to find original interwar locomotives and passenger stock unaffected by metal fatigue. This does mean that pieces in good condition are very sought after, but it can also mean that, unless pieces come from the original owner, components have almost always been replaced. There is now a sizeable industry in Germany making very accurate replica parts; these can be very difficult to detect, particularly when they are inside the mechanism of a locomotive.

The repainting of bodies or fitting of replica parts is doubtless not intended to deceive, but when the piece has changed hands a few times and could be worth a very large sum, potential buyers should be cautious. As a rough guide, modern castings seem a little too heavy, with a slightly lustrous paint finish. The original would look hard and dry. Repainted pieces tend to look too smooth, without the unevenness of the original varnish. Replica wheels usually look too shiny and silver-bright.

Collecting in this field requires considerable research, as there are minute differences between pieces and these can affect value considerably – apart from colour and condition, it is necessary to be aware of details such as coupling type, pantograph type, bogie pattern and number of leaf springs on axles.

below: *The LMS lettering on these factory-overpainted 1937 Märklin coaches can sometimes be quite crooked, but still correct, and the original name can be seen under the paint.*

CONSERVATION AND RESTORATION

Quality toy trains were built to a high standard and the makers may have anticipated hard wear and long service for their products, but probably not that collectors would be clamouring for them so many years later. These treasured possessions now have to be conserved as effectively as possible.

Some locomotives survive with paintwork or lithography intact, in which case they may only need a very light lubrication with sewing-machine oil. Avoid coating paintwork with household oils as they tend to oxidize, leaving a sticky residue that attracts dust.

Problems often occur with good tinplate pieces: the tinning is very smooth and sometimes inadequately primed for the paint finishes, which can flake or peel off, particularly on live-steam locomotives. Both Märklin and Bing can suffer from this problem, so check paintwork carefully. Both can also develop a "craquelure" finish, where the layer of lacquer shrinks in relation to the paint layer beneath, leaving a crazed effect.

Severe damp will destroy even the finest tinplate, but slight moisture over many years can cause spotting or filiform corrosion, a thread-like pattern between metal and paint. Look at pieces all over. A coach in the original box, for instance, may look perfect on the upper side, but have suffered from damp and acidic damage from its box on the lower side. Packaging was not made with archival conservation in mind and is almost always made from acidic wood pulp, which can badly affect paintwork, lithography, lead and diecastings. Wrapping will help, but paper tissues or newspaper are also acidic, so the best materials to use are either top-quality acid-free tissue or a similar quality stiff paper.

Bubble wrap is useful for padding, but never wrap items in it directly, as it can stick firmly, particularly to Märklin lacquer; it is also very flammable. Avoid elastic bands, which stain as they degrade, or sticky tape, which could cause damage when opening the package. If you are packing pieces for shipping, wrap rolls of paper around bogies to stop chafing, and remove and store all loose small parts separately.

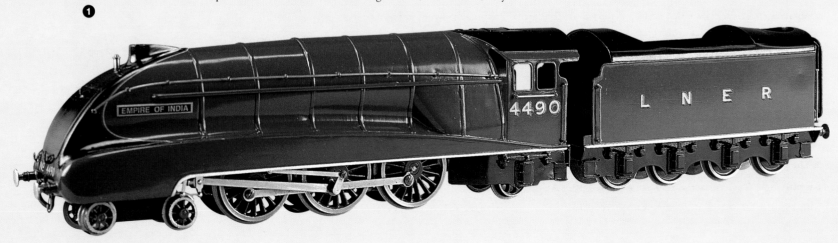

❶

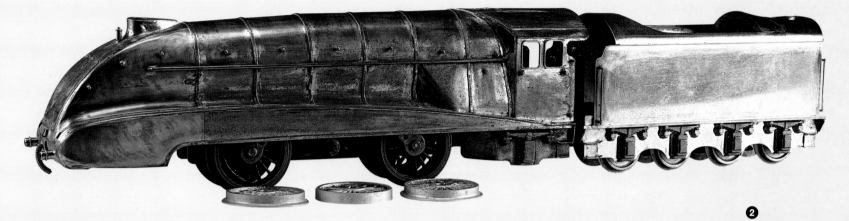

Restoration

There are few more contentious subjects than restoration. As a generalization, British collectors are less keen to have their pieces restored, whereas German and American collectors enjoy seeing pieces revived to pristine condition. No one can deny another person the pleasure of seeing a piece looking new again, but if it is offered for sale, not everyone may share that pleasure – it is so much a question of personal choice. A good example is the Märklin Gauge V train (see page 55), stored for decades in a barn, causing some corrosion to the tinplate and paint flaking to the brass boiler. The train plainly shows its age and reflects its use as a garden railway, but it will remain conserved in this state.

Conservation of loose paint finishes is desirable, as is the removal of obvious denting and the repair of mechanical defects. Work that is badly done with non-reversible materials, however, can damage original finishes for ever, so always use the best restorer available.

1 A Bassett-Lowke LNER A4 "Empress of India", finely repainted by Chris Littledale.
2 The process of restoration is slow and painstaking. This Bassett-Lowke LNER A4 is in the course of being restored, with a replica tender constructed by Chris Littledale.

A piece so well restored that it is hard to spot needs particularly detailed inspection. Fortunately, the best restorers sign their work. Ultraviolet light used in darkness can reveal partial restoration. For example, original Märklin paint and lacquer have a creamy, slightly swirly quality under ultraviolet, whereas new paint shows up as solid purple blocks. Some restorers use synthetic paints on purpose so that their work will show up. Others have now refined their techniques so that new work is very difficult to determine, particularly if the piece has been completely repainted.

A great number of spare parts and transfers are now available, especially for Hornby 0 Gauge and Märklin. Often these are such ephemeral items as flags, but they can include whole body components, so be cautious.

Display

Toy trains look magnificent in showcases. But, like works of art, they should be kept from climatic extremes. Bright sunlight can quickly fade paintwork, especially vulnerable colours such as the LMS lake livery, which deteriorates to a chocolate brown. Indirect natural light or cool artificial light is probably best. Even in protective cabinets, show pieces will still need to be dusted, however airtight the case may seem.

chapter 4

1919–1939

YEARS OF STRUGGLE AND SUCCESS

For most toy train manufacturers the years between the two world wars were a far from easy time, but the era produced some notable and collectible pieces.

BING

Despite the outbreak of war in 1914, Bing was able to produce a fairly full catalogue for Christmas 1915, with an opening section concentrating on military toys. This was the last catalogue issued before 1920, however, and toy production was eventually halted by government decree in 1917 to concentrate on munitions production. Ignatz Bing, co-founder of the company, died in March 1918, and his son Stephan took over as managing director. A combination of Hornby's new 0 Gauge range (see page 118) and anti-German feelings in the export market meant that Bing did not rise to the heights that it had done before the war. Bing's 0 Gauge range had grown smaller and less sophisticated by the end of the 1920s, and the Depression inevitably brought further troubles.

above: The "King Arthur", a beautifully finished steam locomotive for the British market, is equal in quality to previous locomotives made by Bing for Bassett-Lowke.

After World War I, Bing offered a limited range of Gauge I models but kept a wide 0 Gauge range that was well priced for different market segments. Being so reliant on exports, the company suffered badly by comparison with Märklin, but it continued to supply large quantities of material under contract to Bassett-Lowke as well as producing its own "freelance" designs. These were often not so carefully designed or constructed but, being cheaper, often proved much more popular.

Bing produced for Bassett-Lowke a fine hand-painted model of Maunsell's SR 4–6–0 "King Arthur" – the live-steam example pictured above is, remarkably, unused. In 1928 it cost seven times as much as Bing's own 0 Gauge version of the same locomotive which, with its powerful clockwork motor and a lithographed tinplate body, is toy-like in comparison.

Although much was a continuation of pre-war Henry Greenly designs, in 1921 Bing produced for Bassett-Lowke a new range of bogie passenger coaches, known helpfully as 1921 stock, in the Great Western, London North Western and Midland liveries. These were quickly outdated after 1 January 1923, when the rambling British railway network was reorganized. What had been many small companies (see page 181) were reformed into the Big Four: the Great Western Railway (GWR, nicknamed God's Wonderful Railway or Great Way Round), London and North Eastern Railway (LNER, or Late and Never Early Railway), London Midland and Scottish (LMS, or Let Me Sleep) and Southern Railway (SR, or Such Rubbish).

Between 1926 and 1929, the toy versions had their lithography revised and were all reissued in the new liveries. They were sold in distinctive dark-blue boxes with white paper edging and descriptive end labels. An unusual interim version appeared in 1926 when lithographed GWR coaches were overpainted in SR green, pending the issue of the lithographed variant in 1929.

Bing's attempts to export to America faded out through the 1920s in the face of fierce competition, but it had tried hard with models such as the 3238 Bo-Bo high-voltage electric New York Central Electric Tunnel

Locomotive, current from 1920 to 1924. In line with American taste it had a cast iron body, which gave it a suitably solid appearance.

By the late 1920s Bing's buildings and accessories were becoming either flimsy or rather plain in appearance. One of the most pleasing pieces from this time is the hand-painted station, No. 10/6168, which evokes very well the feeling of a sleepy Bavarian market town. Another captivating toy was the Dockyard Traversing Crane (No. 10/685), designed for unloading wagons.

below: *The hand-painted windcutters were the mainstay of Bing's Gauge I quality production for its Continental customers. This is number 11/226 from 1922.*

Bing's greatest coup was the introduction of the new tabletop system in 1922, in conjunction with Bassett-Lowke. Wenman Bassett-Lowke and Henry Greenly took the credit for first planning a tabletop railway in 1914, and Bing, Märklin, Carette and Schönner had all experimented with miniature railways before the war, but world

events prevented further work, and this was the first time that a flexible and affordable system had been produced. The idea was based around lightweight lithographed tinplate locomotives and rolling stock, powered by tiny clockwork motors, running on track half the size of 0 Gauge, which became known as 00 Gauge. Much of the credit must go to Oswald Fischer, the brilliant engineer who actually designed the system, and who later created the Trix Twin system (see page 110).

below: *The 1924 green and gold Bassett-Lowke "Peckett" is always a favourite; perhaps the saddle-tank makes it look rather cuddly.*

The tabletop layout was specifically made for the British market, with representations of tank and tender locomotives and stock from the Big Four railway companies, and proved a big seller until Bing's closure in 1932. It was offered in the British colonies, America and France, but the British origins of the design were only thinly disguised, and it met with little success. It was not even released in Germany until 1924 and never proved very popular there.

In Britain, Gamages were major retailers of the system, rebranding it as their own, and it was sold through Rees & Co – Bing's wholesaler – Bond's o' Euston Road and, of course, Bassett-Lowke. In 1924 the tank locomotives received tiny electric motors, which could run with a regulator or current reducer. Sets were available in all price ranges, from the No. 1 set, comprising clockwork tank locomotive, three coaches and track, to the No. 9 which also contained a station, signal cabin, island platform, level crossing, tunnel, engine shed, buffer stop, signals and telegraph poles.

The 1928 Bing catalogue for the British market does display a useful range of 0 Gauge locomotives and stock, although most are of lightweight quality compared with the golden years before World War I; the three-car electric Metropolitan sets are now popular.

Bing was still capable of producing elegant steam locomotives. The 18-volt electric 0 Gauge Pacific and Tender (No. 11/8105/0) has the sad distinction of being one of the last new designs from the factory; it was issued in 1930, only two years before production ceased. Ironically, its modern American-style high splashers are reminiscent of British Railways' Riddles Standard locomotives of 1951. The "C" Pantograph Electric Locomotive is from the same era, introduced in 1929, and shares a similar six-coupled mechanism to the Pacific. Both locomotives carried on into the Karl Bub stable after the closure of Bing.

Bing was finally forced into receivership on 24 August 1932, but lingered on, selling old stock into 1934. After a

disagreement with the board, Stephan Bing had left the family business in 1927 and had moved to Britain in 1938, following his son Franz who had already emigrated there in 1932. Bing father and son were warmly received by Wenman Bassett-Lowke and some of their descendants still live in Britain today.

W.J. BASSETT-LOWKE & CO.

The years after World War I brought great opportunities to Bassett-Lowke, but great challenges as well. Although anti-German sentiment helped the British toy industry, it was not such an asset for Wenman Bassett-Lowke. He relied on German manufacturers for much of his production, but was fortunate in having a virtual monopoly on wealthy clients. His love of architecture and design was expressed in his house at 78 Derngate, Northampton; between 1916 and 1920 it was remodelled by the great Scottish architect, Charles Rennie Mackintosh, who also designed catalogue artwork and advertising material for the company. Although Mackintosh did not die until 1928, this was his last architectural commission.

When Frank Hornby launched his new 0 Gauge range in June 1920, he aimed at the middle market with a well-made, simple product. At first, it was not direct competition for Bassett-Lowke, but the business expanded as Hornby explored the potential of the range, and sales were boosted by a buying trend away from products of German origin. The bulk of Bassett-Lowke's affordable 0 Gauge range at this time came from Bing, and moves were afoot to ensure that all German imports were marked, but a compromise was reached so that discreet box labelling sufficed. At the same time, however, Bassett-Lowke was holding unsold pre-war stock of Gauge I and II pieces for many years, which is why this material remained in the catalogue for so long.

One of the opening shots in Bassett-Lowke's reinvigorated attack on the post-war market in 1921 was the ubiquitous "Precursor" Tank Locomotive. Another was the little 0–4–0 "Peckett" Tank Locomotive of 1924, produced using old pre-war Carette tooling (see opposite).

The next series, in 1925, started a line that has lasted, on and off, until the present day. The 2–6–0 Moguls were plain but dignified locomotives with six-wheel tenders, designed by Robert Bindon Blood, managing director of Winteringhams, one of Bassett-Lowke's subsidiaries (see page 108). The 0 Gauge LMS and LNER versions are not

above: *The Bassett-Lowke Mogul from 1925 wasn't a very accurate model, but was attractive in unscorched GWR livery.*

top left: *The 1925 Gauge I Mogul had an air of grandeur and proper scale that was missing from the 0 Gauge version (see page 101).*

above: *The graceful lines of Stanier's top link non-streamlined 1933 LMS Princess Coronation class were captured far better by Bassett-Lowke than by Hornby.*

left: *"Flying Scotsman" may be the most famous locomotive of all time. In 1933 Robert Bindon Blood created a tinprinted masterpiece for Bassett-Lowke.*

scarce today, but the GWR and SR versions are less common (see page 101). Although each variant had differences in detailing, the use of common parts kept the price down. They were available with clockwork mechanisms in 0 Gauge and with electric or steam mechanisms in 0 Gauge and Gauge I, but only in LMS and LNER livery in the larger size. Somehow, the extra size added greatly to the poise and realism of the model. The smaller version remained in catalogue until the end of production in the 1960s and was then reissued by Bassett-Lowke Railways Ltd in 1968. Today a noteworthy new version is being made in China under the auspices of Corgi, the present owners of the brand name.

below: *The famous LNER "Footballers" were well represented by the fine Bassett-Lowke "Arsenal" from 1936 – even down to the football on the nameplate.*

In June 1927, Bassett-Lowke announced a competitively priced clockwork lithographed 4–4–0 locomotive and tender, the "Duke of York", with newly designed Winteringham bodies. The novel part was that it could either be bought outright, or exchanged for Godfrey Phillips BDV cigarette coupons. During its five-year production run, the tenders were numbered 1927, 1930 and 1931. It was highly successful, but a tight contract meant

that it was still not a profitable venture. Nevertheless, it used up quantities of Bing parts, and from it came a 4–6-volt electric version in January 1928, followed by "Princess Elizabeth" in 1932 and "Prince Charles" in 1951.

Between 1929 and 1938, Bassett-Lowke produced its most famous and sought-after range of 0 Gauge locomotives, again under the auspices of Robert Bindon Blood. The lithographed LMS 4–6–0 "Royal Scot" was the first to appear; a well-detailed model of the original, it was far in advance of any comparable product and came with a Fowler tender. The tender seems quite upright and antiquated by comparison with the 1939 model that accompanied the more modern and sleeker Stanier version; it is also distinguished by having a painted finish with smoke deflectors on each side of the smokebox.

In 1933 Blood's model of a most famous locomotive appeared: the LNER 4–6–2 "Flying Scotsman". Available in clockwork or electric versions, it was another masterpiece of lithography, in the LNER's smart green livery. The Hornby 20-volt electric "Flying Scotsman" was half the price, but was very clearly a toy, while the Bassett-Lowke version had model-like pretensions. The lines of

the original were well recreated and it was mounted on the correct six-coupled wheel set, with a bogie corridor tender added. Its success can be judged by the fact that it was still in the Bassett-Lowke catalogue twenty-five years later.

The first of Sir William Stanier's earlier, non-streamlined LMS Princess Coronation class to leave Crewe works in 1933 was No. 6200, "Princess Royal", but the most famous is undoubtedly No. 6201, "Princess Elizabeth", which first appeared in 1935 and is rare. Once again, the later Hornby "Princess Elizabeth" is found wanting by comparison with the plainer Bassett-Lowke; although it lacks lining, the elegant lines are better realized (see page 103).

Another fetching and scarce model came out in 1936; the originals, derived from the LNER 4-6-0 "Sandringham" class, were named after football teams and were known as the "Footballers". The Bassett-Lowke model of "Arsenal" (see left) accurately modelled the football under the nameplate, above the centre splasher, and is very scarce today.

Most enthusiasts, if asked to select the most glamorous locomotives of the late 1930s, would light on two streamlined classes that regularly competed with each other – the LMS Princess Coronations of Sir William Stanier and the LNER A4s of Sir Nigel Gresley (see above and page 106).

Bassett-Lowke modelled the A4s in seven names and liveries and the Coronations in two names and liveries; they are almost certainly among the most alluring model locomotives ever made in Britain. Despite the number of variants that could be bought, they were an expensive purchase and seem to have sold in only small numbers.

Today, good examples will fetch substantial prices – if they can be found at all. Nevertheless, the manufacturing process was sometimes surprisingly crude, with internal component sections cut out roughly and soldered together. With some filler and paint added, the result looked superb, but the roughness beneath the surface means they are not without conservation problems. Inadequate removal of soldering flux can result in corrosion between the surface of the tinplate and the paint layer, and poor priming before painting can lead to flaking. As a result, these locomotives are very hard to find today in fine, original condition, and it is more common to find examples that have been either partially or completed repainted.

above: *The streamlined LMS "Coronation" from c. 1938: now almost impossible to find in untouched condition, it is very valuable.*

1

"SIR NIGEL GRESLEY" LOCOMOTIVES

The Hornby-Dublo "Sir Nigel Gresley" locomotive, introduced in 1938, was a tribute to the legendary chief mechanical engineer, Sir Nigel Gresley. No. 4498 was available as clockwork (DL1) or electric (EDL1), both finished in the attractive LNER blue livery. Because of the deep valance below the splashers covering the wheels, it was not thought necessary to reproduce the valve gear in detail.

Pre-war models with the full skirts are rare. The EDL1 was only available for just under two years and the DL1 for just over three; in practice, few were sold after 1940. The wheel skirts were removed from the real locomotives for ease of maintenance during World War II; Hornby-Dublo did the same on post-war models, which is the simplest way of telling the two versions apart. The pre-war range was also fitted with a unique tensile steel flat hook coupling. It was slim and smoothly styled, but didn't work very well. After World War II it was replaced with the more successful Peco patent coupling.

Both versions were marvels of miniaturization, powerful enough to head trains of respectable size, and smooth and quiet runners, with less gear noise than Trix locomotives. Although

tiny, the clockwork mechanism would run all the way round a typical 2.5 x 1.2m (8 x 4ft) layout. One of the challenges of running such a clockwork train is to start it at a station, having wound the locomotive with the precise number of turns that halts it again at exactly the same spot; quite a number of wagers have been lost in this game.

Although they were intended for non-electrified homes, the clockwork locomotives were not very popular at the time. They were not cheap – Hornby's much larger 0 Gauge clockwork No. 2 Special Tank Locomotive cost less – and their sleek lines were spoiled by two large control levers sticking out through the cab roof. On the plus side, they ran on two-rail track, which looked more realistic than the three-rail version.

The locomotives are now rare, particularly in their original boxes. Apart from the printing, the boxes for both the electric and the clockwork versions are the same, solidly constructed from card covered in pale blue paper and all dated 9.38, except for a box for a separate tender.

The curse of metal fatigue attacks the Hornby-Dublo range as severely as any other mazac Meccano products. Fortunately, pieces that have survived this long are unlikely to

decay further provided that they are kept in stable environmental conditions. The bodies and the bogie frames of the A4s, being made of tinplate, are usually sound, but the wheels and sub-frames tend to suffer. Very slight expansion of the mazac means that the wheels drop off the axles or that the cotter pins securing the coupling rods to the driving wheels fall out. The dummy coal deck was made of a plastic material that tends to warp.

1 **For comparison, a Bassett-Lowke model of Sir Nigel Gresley's three-rail electric 0 Gauge LNER A4 "Empress of India", showing the pre-war full skirts.**
2 **The post-war Hornby-Dublo version of the "Sir Nigel Gresley". The pre-war version of the locomotive had full skirts fitted (see page 147).**

above: *The GWR "King George V": a magical combination of lustrous paintwork and body by Märklin with a Bassett-Lowke mechanism.*

To replace the work formerly done by Bing, Märklin built five locomotives for Bassett-Lowke between 1934 and 1937, to the designs of Henry Greenly. The Märklin craftsmen brought their own special recipe of heavy-gauge tinplate and thick, lustrous paint finish to Greenly's work, producing some locomotives of great beauty and appeal. In some cases Bassett-Lowke mechanisms were used, if their wheels were closer to scale or DC motors were required. The GWR 4–6–0 "King George V" from 1935 to 1936 (above) is probably the most desirable model of the group, combining traditional appearance with modern performance. Also charming, in its own way, is the Märklin model of Stanier's sturdy 2–6–4 LMS Tank Locomotive, which was on sale from 1935 to 1937. The British have a particular affection for tank locomotives, even if they are in a grimy and weatherbeaten condition.

Another curiosity marketed by Bassett-Lowke was a British version of the famous Märklin train, "Der Adler", introduced in 1935 to celebrate the centenary of the first German railway. It differed from the German version only by the absence of the "Der Adler" lettering on the locomotive boiler (see page 84).

With fewer components being supplied by German companies, Bassett-Lowke pieces were increasingly being manufactured by Winteringhams, the company Wenman Bassett-Lowke and George Winteringham had started back in 1908, and which was now part of the Bassett-Lowke "family" in Northampton. Through the Winteringhams connection, Bassett-Lowke made good use of the ex-Carette tooling, particularly for the twelve-wheel dining car, which was issued in plain LMS lake livery. With the running down and eventual demise of Bing in August 1932, Winteringhams had to build up its own range of 0 Gauge passenger stock, which it did between 1930 and 1934. It produced mainline 1st Class

and 3rd/Brake coaches in the liveries of each of the Big Four rail companies, as well as two LMS Suburban Coaches and an LMS Travelling Post Office. The post office was another ex-Carette piece, and Bassett-Lowke also sold the ground gear on plinth that allowed this novel vehicle to work its pick-up hook and catching net for mail sacks. It also made a very collectible LMS Watford–Euston Suburban Electric Multiple Unit.

Despite Winteringhams' best efforts, it could not rival the superb modern coaching stock made by Edward Exley for Bassett-Lowke. Although only made of hand-painted and lettered aluminium over a wooden sub-frame, Exley's pieces (see right) look magnificent hauled behind a top link locomotive.

The "Mobiloil" and "Esso" tank wagons made in 1935 by Winteringhams are very collectible in fine condition. The Hornby Series "Colas" and "United Dairies" Milk Tank Wagons are similar in form but seem almost crudely robust compared to the delicate lithography on the Winteringham tanks, which even give maximum tare details on the wagon chassis.

In contrast to the use of lithography elsewhere in their production, Bassett-Lowke continued to make lineside buildings out of painted wood (see page 110). Pieces left on attic layouts tend to deteriorate quickly, so Bassett-Lowke buildings from this time rarely survive in a pristine state. In addition to stations engine sheds, signal cabins, kiosks and a platelayer's hut were also available. Other typical accessories included platform furniture, turntables, buffer stops, signal lever frames and good-quality brass track with wooden sleepers. Some of the most coveted additions to any layout were packets of miniature tinplate signs, in imitation of the enamelled iron signs that used to be found on railway buildings. Bassett-Lowke buildings came ready dressed, but the extra signs could be used elsewhere for added realism. Some are now scarce and

below: *No other British maker rivalled Exley's detailed bogie coaches; they perfectly complement Bassett-Lowke locomotives.*

bottom: *For more mundane use, the Märklin's Stanier tank made from 1935 to 1937 for Bassett-Lowke still looks elegant.*

creation of the company there, so it can really be considered Anglo-German.

Stephan Bing resigned as managing director of the family firm in 1927. The following year he bought an established toy and lead-figure manufacturer and was able to take some key colleagues from Bing with him. The first new product in 1930–31 was a construction toy called Trix, made up of perforated steel plates of various shapes and sizes. It was sufficiently successful that Stephan Bing soon looked to overseas expansion, and in early 1932 he set up a new company, Trix Ltd, in Britain, with his old friend Wenman Bassett-Lowke as co-director. At the same time, production of the construction toy started under licence at Winteringhams.

One can now only speculate, but possibly inspired by Bassett-Lowke, a team in Nürnberg developed a new three-rail electric 00 Gauge railway system during 1933 and 1934. It was headed by Siegfried Kahn, ex-Bing technical manager, with most of the design input once again coming from Oswald Fischer, who had designed Bing's tabletop system.

Trix Express was launched in March 1935 at the Leipzig Toy Fair and was an immediate success. The range consisted of Deutsche Reichsbahn goods and passenger sets, rolling stock and accessories. The locomotives had sturdy four-wheel mechanisms, with coarse scale mazac wheels with thick tyres. The track on which the new range ran was also of an entirely new and ingenious design, with steel rail mounted on a Bakelite base that was moulded to give an impression of sleepers and ballast. Each piece clicked into the next, with the third-rail contacts sprung to ensure effective contact. In practice, if the geometry of a layout is not perfect, it tends to come apart; it also rusts quite freely.

very collectible. Much more eccentric are a small group of solid lead figures that Bassett-Lowke commissioned from Heyde in Dresden. They represent prominent figures of the era, including Bassett-Lowke himself, Lloyd George, George Bernard Shaw, Amy Johnson and Charlie Chaplin.

TRIX TWIN AND TRIX EXPRESS

The history of Trix is extraordinarily complex, with a business family tree that resembles a bowl of spaghetti. Although the original company was founded in Germany, it had always had close ties with Britain even prior to the

At the heart of the system was the brilliant new 14-volt AC mechanism. This operated with a common-return centre rail, with controlled current coming from either outside rail via adjustable pick-ups. This meant that two locomotives could be controlled independently on the same section of track, even allowing for head-to-head running. The remote reverse was also a breakthrough: in essence, a button on the controller acted as a circuit breaker which caused a relay to flip and the armature to reverse direction. This was only supposed to take place when the train was stationary, but spectacular sliding reverses could be achieved.

The first sets arrived in Britain in November 1935 and sold out before Christmas. Passenger Set No. 11/2 was entirely German in outline, although it was marketed as The Bassett-Lowke Twin Train Table Railway. An early set can be immediately identified by the use of disc, rather than spoked, wheels.

During 1936, design and production of British Trix Twin started at Winteringhams using German motors, with production ready for Christmas that year. Typical motive power was provided by a No. 5/515 0–4–0 Southern Side-Tank Locomotive, in black freight livery. The same motor provided power for an LMS compound, No. 2/536. The freight stock resembled miniature Winteringham 0 Gauge vehicles, in carefully lithographed finishes. Trix couplings at this time consisted of a mazac hook and sprung wire eye, linked by a tensioning spring on four-wheel vehicles. It worked well in principle, but in practice the hooks tended to break and the wire links fall off – luckily members of the Trix Twin Collectors Association (see page 185) can provide spare parts.

In 1937, Trix introduced a modular station building system designed by E. W. Twining in Northampton; it was called Manyways. The imposing central tower section and some of the smaller parts were of heavy diecast mazac, with other parts made from painted tinplate with wooden roofs. The first buildings offered by Trix in Britain had been imported from Germany, built in painted wood to designs inspired by Ashfield Station (see opposite). For a brief period from late 1936 to mid-1937, a range of Northampton-built painted wooden buildings was available, and these are now very rare. Also on sale was a range of platform figures and accessories to go with the buildings.

The vast majority of pre-war boys owning Trix Twin trains either had these tank locomotives or similar tender locomotives, with freight or passenger stock in single or double sets. The four-wheel coaches were disappointingly

below: *Three variations of attractive self-promotion are painted on 0 Gauge open wagons. Made in 1912, 1924 and 1935.*

above: A 00 Gauge dream present for Christmas 1938: Trix and Bassett-Lowke together produced at great expense a brace of top link locomotives in fine presentation cases.

toy-like and the ordinary bogie coaches were little better. They were well lithographed but were very out of scale, as was the standard mechanism in the motor bogie coach.

An extremely lucky boy would have had one of the two prestige sets of 1938: the LNER (Flying) "Scotsman" (No. 4/344) or the LMS "Princess" (Elizabeth) (No. 2/344), which included much more satisfactory coaches that were closer to the correct scale all around and as long as possible for the track radius. Bassett-Lowke imported complete DR Pacifics from Germany, then threw away the bodies, putting on their own. They came in lined, rexine-covered cases, with three of the finest Northampton-made Trix coaches.

For the same price, the luckiest boy of all in 1939 would have received the finest Trix Twin set made – the No. 2/437 "Coronation" (see opposite). Of the company's grand ideas, it was one of the few to come to fruition in the troubled months before World War II, but was a fitting note to go out on. The design captured beautifully the lines of Sir William Stanier's streamlined Princess Coronation locomotives. It came equipped with bell and headlamp, as fitted to the "Duchess of Hamilton" disguised as the "Coronation" when she went over to the New York World's Fair in the same year. The All 1st and Brake/3rd coaches in the set were slightly adapted regular scale-length coaches with special striped paint detail, "Coronation Scot" nameboards and streamlined panels below the chassis. The overall effect was remarkable, but sales did not reach the hoped for 1,000 units, partly because of the success of Hornby-Dublo (see page 142), whose EDP1 "Sir Nigel Gresley" set was half the price of Trix's "Coronation" set.

Two further rarities appeared under the Trix name before the war, neither easily available in Britain at the time. The first was a curious hybrid, created at the end of 1937 at the instigation of Monsieur Gaston Gobin-Daudé, Trix agent in Paris. It was a 4–4–0 locomotive, No. 22/56, representing a Nord Pacific, designed by Chapelon (see opposite), probably the greatest of all steam-locomotive engineers. The motor came from Germany and the tender bogies from Northampton, with the locomotive and coach bodies cast locally in France. It is now extremely scarce and more often found as a good-quality modern replica.

The second was Trix Express No. 9/186 from 1939: a freelance German-outline Pacific adapted for the American market with some detail changes, including the inevitable fitting of a cowcatcher, removal of the smoke deflectors and white banding to the locomotive body and tender. Few were sold, and it is thus a great rarity today.

LIONEL

By the early 1920s, the Lionel Line, which had dominated the American market before World War I, was beginning to have a rather antiquated look. The company had divided into two major spheres of influence: Mario Caruso and his largely first-generation Italian immigrants manufactured the trains in Irvington, New Jersey, and Lionel Cowen and his friends and relatives handled the sales administration offices in New York. Caruso had engineering connections in his native Italy, and a company was set up in Naples to design and make the dies and machinery for the new Lionel trains.

The first locomotive designed in Italy was yet another NYC S3 electric loco, but it had shiny brass details such as axle boxes and handrails and was painted an attractive light brown – in fact, the same shade of brown used by the electric locomotives in Italy. No US locomotives were ever painted light brown, but that did not seem to matter and the locomotive was enthusiastically received. The new Lionel Line featured deep embossing, brass name plaques and details and bright colours such as peacock blue for the refrigerator car, introduced at long last.

Freight cars came in two different sizes in Standard Gauge and two different sizes in 0 Gauge. Passenger cars came in several sizes and the de-luxe ones had removable roofs and interior details. Electric locomotives were also made in the Milwaukee Olympian style in both Standard and 0 Gauge, as well as in the boxy New Haven types. New steam engines were offered in both gauges and the top of the line, Standard Gauge 4–4–4, was the eye-popping "Blue Comet", with matching brilliant blue coaches. It was not very realistic, but what a toy! Even larger was the giant Standard Gauge Olympian electric outline 4–4–4, which pulled the huge "California" coaches. Bold and beautiful, these two trains epitomized the extravagant spirit of the Roaring Twenties. Fortunately for collectors,

below: Two of the great Trix rarities: the British streamlined 1939 LMS Princess Coronation Pacific and (bottom) a shortened French version of Chapelon's Nord Pacific from 1937. Both locomotives came with specially designed coaches and are very valuable today.

the construction was very simple and the Lionel Company has remanufactured both of these sets in recent years. Collectors love them but the innocent days, when American children dreamed of being the president of their own railroad, have long gone. A year before the Wall Street crash, at the height of the boom, the poorly managed and long shaky Ives Company went under and Lionel, along with American Flyer and Dorfan, bought the remains. Lionel continued the name and even brought new, middle-rank, trains on to the market under the Ives name. After a short while these trains were rebranded as Lionel, but the Depression struck and the lifespan of these trains was short. Collectors are interested in limited issues and consequently there is considerable interest in the Ives–Lionel transition period.

below: *The 1937 Lionel "scale Hudson", manufactured in both 0 and 00 Gauge, gave Lionel a great deal of prestige but did not earn much money for the company.*

right: *Lionel's "Hell Gate Bridge" from 1928 was cleverly designed. Its lack of ramps provided a large bridge that did not need much space.*

The Depression brought a sharp change in Lionel's fortunes. Die-making became cheaper in the USA and new trains were designed using high-pressure zamac (as mazac was called in the United States) die-castings for the frames. Steam locomotives began to replace the electrics. The Depression deepened and Lionel went into receivership, only to be saved by a brilliant new train, the 0 Gauge

Union Pacific M10000. This was a realistic scale model painted bright yellow and brown. People loved "Streamliners" in the depressed 1930s — they looked so modern and seemed to offer hope for a brighter tomorrow. The M10000 was followed by a variation of the "Burlington Zephyr" called the "Flying Yankee", with a chrome finish. An exciting "Hiawatha" followed, and there was also the "Commodore Vanderbilt" and a very fine "City of Denver".

Amid all this new excitement, Standard Gauge quietly died, and then came three different sizes of 0 Gauge, each differentiated by a number indicating the track radius: 027 for track with a radius of 27in (68cm), 072 for a 72-in (1.83-m) radius, and 0 for the "standard" track, which fell between the other two in size.

In the late 1930s, the steam-outline locomotives began to acquire diecast superstructures, and Lionel made a couple of brave, but ill-fated, ventures into scale-model railroading. For the 0 Gauge enthusiast, Lionel created a very fine diecast replica of the famous NYC 4–6–4 "Hudson". The locomotive was marketed in various forms: full scale with wooden plinth, a less detailed version called semi-scale and a build-it-yourself kit. To match this fine engine were four exceptional freight cars: a boxcar, tank car, hopper car and caboose. A scale 0–6–0

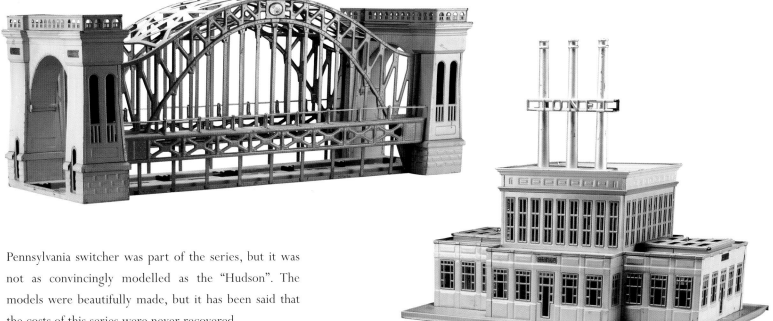

Pennsylvania switcher was part of the series, but it was not as convincingly modelled as the "Hudson". The models were beautifully made, but it has been said that the costs of this series were never recovered.

Another development was the 00 system, which used 00 track and correct proportions, resulting in a slightly larger scale than British 00 Gauge. It featured a smaller "Hudson" and a limited number of diecast freight cars. In common with the 0 Gauge range, there was no refrigerator car – an echo of earlier Lionel days. Once, again, build-it yourself kits were also offered. Although it was relatively popular at the end of the 1930s, 00 Gauge lost out to the smaller H0 Gauge and Lionel abandoned its small-gauge effort in 1942.

Before the 1920s, Lionel's accessories had been the usual ones most toy companies supplied: a station, buffer stops, lamps, passenger footbridge, signals and so on. Things began to change in the 1930s and Lionel started to manufacture an astonishing range. Operating accessories became a Lionel speciality, and its Bascule Bridge was spectacular. The Hell Gate Bridge (above) was a superb idea for a bridge; it required no ramps, took up minimum

room, looked like the prototype and had sufficient height to impress. Then there was the Powerhouse Station – at 45cm (18in) high and 66cm (26in) wide, this was a huge building for a toy train set-up – and the Terraced Station, which provided a wonderful platform for figures and really did suggest a large terminal station. There was also a truly massive, all-metal Corner Tunnel, a range of small houses, operating log loaders, iceing platforms and crossing gates (complete with a guard who pops out of the hut when the train goes by). For a brief time a sectional Round House was marketed, which would take Standard Gauge locomotives. Each section was 60cm (24in) at the back, and a four-section semi-circle made up probably the largest toy railway structure ever catalogued.

above: *The Lionel Powerhouse was a very large building and could be used to hide the transformer. It was introduced in 1928.*

chapter 5

1920–1941

THE STORY OF HORNBY

When World War I ended in November 1918, the political and economic landscape of Europe looked very different from the sunnier days of August 1914. After the death and injury of many millions of men, the empires of Russia and Germany had fallen and Britain's wealth had been fatally weakened. The enmity created by slaughter on an industrial scale and the flawed Treaty of Versailles in 1919 helped to create the poisoned atmosphere of the interwar years. Old cross-border business partnerships in the toy world were revived, but in a more muted fashion. Anglo-German relations were not the same and a spirit of nationalism made buyers more wary of goods stamped "Foreign".

It was against this background of nationalism that the toy train business of Hornby was born. Frank Hornby was no stranger to the business of toys: the construction kits he had invented in 1901– originally labelled Mechanics Made Easy, but soon known to the world as Meccano – had already made him a millionaire. Unlike Wenman Bassett-Lowke, Frank Hornby always prided himself on producing his own material wherever possible, and all the company's pressing of tinplate sheet, casting and painting was carried out at the Hornby Binns Road factory in Liverpool.

Frank Hornby had also learned from the designs of Märklin and Bing. As early as 1912 he had received a patent for a railway-based novelty game called Raylo (see above). It involved speedily diverting a clockwork locomotive via points levers around two interlinked ovals of track on a large wood and steel plinth, with disaster looming if levers were not thrown correctly. The internal components were partly made from old Mechanics Made Easy components, with Meccano pattern threads, bosses, axles and nuts. It seems likely that it was built in house, but its origin cannot be definitely stated. The little 0–4–0 locomotive was one of the Märklin Lilliput series, made from 1912 onwards – another of the many links between the two companies before World War I.

In June 1920, Hornby launched his new 0 Gauge clockwork railway system. He saw it as an extension of the Meccano principle, which was based on a number of drilled nickel-plated plates, girders and wheels of standardized form which could be mass-produced and used to create models in infinite varieties, armed only with nuts, bolts, tools and endless patience.

Like Meccano constructor oufits, the new Hornby trains were sold largely through local shops. A town's main street then was full of independent retailers rather than the chains that today make shopping streets in Guildford, Lyons or Milan virtually indistinguishable. Those that had the sole local agency for Hornby Trains and Meccano usually sold its products alongside the rubbery aroma of bicycles and the crackle of acoustic gramophones.

The locomotives in Hornby's first train sets had a solid and naïve charm. Two versions were offered – a cheap Tinprinted Clockwork Train copied completely from a small Bing locomotive and tender with matching coaches, and the more substantial Hornby Clockwork Train; this latter was to form the basis of the Hornby railway system. The Hornby Clockwork Train locomotives had plain painted metal bodies, overscale fittings (the handrails along the boiler were the scale thickness of drainpipes), undersized four-wheel mechanisms and brass buffers and coupling hooks. The open wagons in the first set were as plain and solid as the locomotive, with un-ornamented sides and sub-frames held together with nuts and bolts, thick plated metal axles and brass couplings and buffers from the locomotives.

The locomotives were originally issued in the colours of three of the old railway companies – Great Northern, Midland, and London and North Western. The wagons were all painted grey, but different white capital letters were tabbed on to each vehicle, depending on the company. The set came in a red box with an ambitious label showing a GCR 4–6–0 heading an express passenger train, although it was soon changed to a brown box with decoratively embossed lid, with a diagram of all the components on the inside. A passenger set followed in 1921,

and the locomotive was improved with a new mechanism and finer fittings. The coaches were box-like, with four wheels and plain liveries. They did, however, feature separately applied doors with brass lettering, celluloid windows and a more detailed underframe. Liveries now included Caledonian, with a classy blue locomotive, and LB&SCR.

Hornby realized that the constructional style of his models could not compare in a similar price range with the cheaper, tabbed construction of Bing and other makes. As early as 1921, Hornby introduced a bogie locomotive in the form of a 4–4–0 (see below), with bogie coaches to accompany it. It was followed by a cheaper version of the 0–4–0 – the "Zulu", only available in black – and, soon after, an 0–4–0 tank locomotive and the very handsome No. 2 4–4–4 tank locomotive.

The early wagon base gave way in 1922 to a lighter frame with pierced axle guards, and was followed by transferred, rather than tabbed, railway company insignia, clearly displayed "Hornby Series" transfers, thin axles and more sophisticated drop-link couplings. New and more adventurous models included the private owner vans. In railway practice at the time, these vans were owned by the

below: Introduced to the Hornby 0 Gauge range in 1921, the 4–4–0s brought a little more realism to the range.

companies themselves and formed an important part of long mixed-freight trains, which used to grumble and wheeze between vast marshalling yards, with incoming stock shunted into newly arranged trains to continue their journey. "Colman's Mustard" was the first – and now the most valuable – Hornby private owner van, only produced from 1923 to 1924. Decorated with gaudy transfers, the bright yellow paintwork is very fragile, so mint examples are almost impossible to find. It was replaced by a new series of vans: "Seccotine" (a type of glue), "Crawford's Biscuits", "Jacob & Co's Biscuits" and "Carr's Biscuits". Boxed examples of all these in excellent condition are much sought after by collectors; furthermore, their bold colours make a fine display running on a layout.

By 1925, the Hornby Series had grown enormously, prompting Meccano to issue the annual *Hornby Book of Trains*. In keeping with the educational feel of the company, the first twenty-two pages of the book contained details of new locomotives, technical detail and history designed to enthral the budding young engineer. The next twenty-two pages contained the "hard sell": they detail the enormous effort and investment Hornby was putting into its growing range. The original locomotive was called the No. 1, with its tank engine equivalent, while the 4–4–0 and the 4–4–4T were called the No. 2 and No. 2 Tank Locomotive. Rolling stock included two bogie Pullman coaches, four-wheel clerestory-roof coaches in LMS and LNER liveries and a large range of wagons. These included a snow plough with operating fan blade,

left: *Private owner vans, milk tank wagons and the bitumen tank wagons (see page 137) are the most desirable freight wagons in the Hornby range. The "Colman's Mustard" van was the first in the series and is now the rarest; its original box is even scarcer.*

gunpowder vans, petrol tank wagon and various bogie vans and wagons. They were accompanied by a growing range of accessories (see page 138) that had begun with the constructional footbridge in 1921.

By this time, all Hornby items came packaged in bright red boxes with illustrations of their contents printed on the end flaps, an important marketing development and a first for a British or Continental manufacturer. As a result, Hornby boxes are highly valued by collectors today and significantly add to the value of their contents.

A significant introduction in 1926 was the Control System, which merited a separate folder. It provided the opportunity to construct a realistic layout, with the miniature signal cabin copying the functions of the full-sized prototype. Using similar principles, the cabin contained a miniature lever frame, connected by rods to the signals and points, although it was not a genuine interlock system. The Control System linkage was achieved through various guides and rotating connectors, using wires trimmed to length with a pair of snips. Although simple in principle, the system was quite expensive when new and was not a great success; therefore it is sought after by collectors today.

Two new prestige sets featured in the 1926 *Book of Trains*, both available in electric as well as clockwork. One represented a rather unusual prototype for the British market, although less so in the growing French market: the famous Wagons-Lits "Riviera Blue" train that ran from Calais to the Mediterranean (see page 122). It conveyed the rich of northern Europe from chillier climes to the fashionable warmth of the Côte d'Azur, at a time when only the wealthy took foreign holidays. Its name was made on 13 March 1930, when Woolf Barnato, the "Bentley

Boy", raced the train from Cannes in his Bentley 6.5-litre Speed Six Saloon; he arrived in London four minutes before the train arrived in Calais.

The "Riviera Blue" set was a luxury item. It featured a fair representation of a locomotive from the Nord, one of the French pre-nationalization rail companies, albeit in Atlantic rather than the correct Pacific form. It was finished in brown livery with gold lining and lettering. The eight-wheel bogie coaches were in dark blue livery, with gold lettering identifying them as sleeping cars and dining cars. The windows were glazed with a strip of celluloid showing interior detail; this

above: The Hornby Control system was a novel mechanical solution imitating real running practice, using linking rods.

tends to warp with age. In true Hornby toy-like style, the cream-painted roofs were secured by four hugely out-of-scale circular brass nuts.

The other prestige set had been introduced in 1925, at the time of the second British Empire Exhibition at Wembley, and in some ways was even more unusual than the "Riviera Blue". It was a current Metropolitan Railway locomotive and non-corridor 1st Class and Brake/3rd coaches, and was at first available only in high-voltage form (see page 123). Although it was supplied with a variable resistor, in short circuit a full-voltage shock could be delivered, so in 1926 Hornby introduced clockwork and low-voltage versions. The high-voltage set is consequently quite rare, but even the 4-volt sets are much sought after by collectors. Although they do not sit comfortably with the rest of the Hornby products, they are good representations of the original range, being lithographed rather than enamelled. Hornby was fortunate to have the services of Ronald Wyborn as electrical engineer from the beginning to end of the original company. His designs for electrical equipment were of such quality that many original pieces are still in use today, although they should now be used with great caution and checked by a qualified electrician.

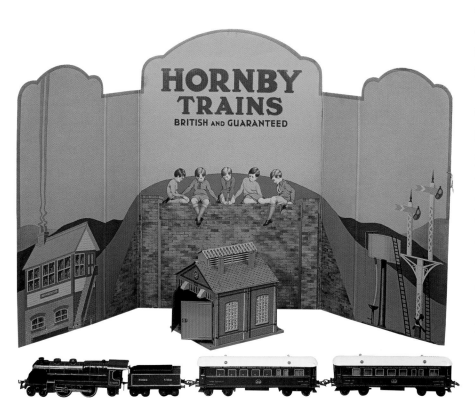

THE "FLYING SCOTSMAN" AND THE LUXURY NO. 3 SETS

The arrival of the "Flying Scotsman" in 1927 marked the beginning of Hornby's finest years, which continued up to the end of toy production in 1941, when factory output turned solely to war work.

Originally built in 1922 as No. 1472, the full-size train was the third A1 Class locomotive to be built in the Doncaster works for the old Great Northern Railway, just prior to the railway system regrouping the following January. She was designed by Sir Nigel Gresley and had a distinctively wide parabolic Wootton firebox that ensured a large grate area, thus producing plenty of steam. Hornby metamorphosed the Nord 4–4–2 into British outline by removing a dome, adding two pairs of dummy splashers and replacing the tender with a six-wheel version that was also used for the No. 2 4–4–0. In this form it was turned out numbered and named as the "Flying Scotsman", the LNER "top shed" locomotive.

The "Royal Scot" represented the LMS, the "Caerphilly Castle" the GWR (see page 125) and, following in 1928, the "Lord Nelson" the SR. This offended purists, but not the child recipients; these models were the apogee of a boy's aspirations at the time and so they proved very popular. Following the established pattern, these engines were called No. 3s and were very good value. Although common today in most forms, unusually the clockwork 1927–8 series is rare compared to the electric equivalent – the reverse of the normal situation.

These locomotives formed the basis of the No. 3 Passenger Sets, which had evocative names: LMS "The

left: *Most small boys in the 1930s did not need this advertising display to help with their Christmas wishes.*

Royal Scot", LNER "The Flying Scotsman" and GWR "Cornish Riviera Express". They are rarely found in excellent and complete condition; the large boxes were very vulnerable and are often found with damage to lid sides or missing interior partitions. All were available as Pullman sets until 1937, with "The Golden Arrow" continuing until 1941.

THE CHEAPER RANGES

At the other end of the financial scale, Hornby offered a range of relatively inexpensive electric and clockwork 0–4–0 tender and tank locomotives. In the 1938 catalogue, the cheapest was the simple lithographed clockwork non-reversing MO Locomotive and Tender, introduced in 1931. It was included in the MO Passenger Train Set with two simple lithographed four-wheel MO Pullman coaches, "Joan" and "Zena", at a tenth of the price of the least expensive of the prestige sets in the same catalogue. Not surprisingly, their price today is even lower in relation to the prestige sets. Even the M11 Complete Model Railway, which included a tank locomotive, three wagons, track, points, tunnel, station, signal and signal cabin, level crossing, footbridge, two trees with stands, a guard, a cow and a horse, is still not much sought after today, despite the fact that it is rarely found complete and in good condition.

Other cheaper locomotives included the M1 locomotive, which looked more realistic than the MO and had a reversing mechanism. There was also the lithographed M3 Tank Locomotive, and the No.1 Tank Locomotive, which had a painted finish and better mechanism; both came in clockwork and electric forms. DC electric versions of these locomotives were sold with a reversing switch and are very rare in Southern livery (see page 127).

The No.1 Special locomotives were the most expensive in the four-wheel range; not only were they in a painted finish, but they had more detail and extra lining. Their main feature was a more powerful four-coupled motor, with larger driving wheels that extended above the footplate in a more realistic fashion. Because the electric No. 1 Specials were little cheaper than the electric No. 2 Specials, they sold in smaller numbers and consequently are sought after today.

above: First introduced in 1925, the London Metropolitan Railway electric locomotives were finely tinprinted.

THE NO. 2 SPECIALS

The mainstay of the Hornby range was the No. 2 Special Tank Locomotive, introduced in 1929 to replace the No. 2 4–4–4 Tank Locomotive. It had a 4–4–2 wheel arrangement, broader diameter boiler, firebox pressing showing wash-out plugs and larger wheels (see page 127). Although it was a less elegant model than the No. 2, the No. 2 Special Tank looked powerful, chunky and modern and sold in huge quantities until it was withdrawn in the 1940s. As before, the LMS version is most often seen, followed by the LNER and GWR, with Southern's black freight livery being rarest of all. As maids of all work, these tank locomotives usually had a hard life on the playroom floor, so, despite their popularity at the time, they are now often in less than excellent condition.

The No. 2 Special Tender Locomotives, also introduced in 1929, generally seem to have been better treated. These were a different species, being true to type, modelled on clearly individual prototypes from each of the Big Four companies. The most common is the LMS version. It is worth remembering that Hornby's LMS lake livery – a deep maroon colour – is a very fugitive finish; it fades badly if exposed to daylight. A serious collector would only be interested in any locomotive if it retained its original factory high-gloss finish, which can usually only be found if the piece has been stored in non-acidic wrapping in the dark for many years. If it has been exposed to daylight and to dirt, the finish is flat and matt, and the colour will have faded to a muddy chocolate brown.

below: This 1930s export freight train is in the livery of the central railway of Argentina, an important market between the wars.

The No. 2 Special Locomotives of the other Big Four companies are among the most desirable and expensive Hornby models that many collectors aspire to own. For most of its production run, the LNER Shire Class "Yorkshire" was only available with a clockwork mechanism, but for just a few months in 1934 to 1935 it was available briefly with a 20-volt electric mechanism (see page 142), before Hornby turned it into a Hunt Class known as "The Bramham Moor", with the distinctive silhouette of a running fox at the top of the nameplate.

Even more popular with collectors is the GWR "County of Bedford", finished in dark green livery and with a short roof to the cab. Hornby also copied the Great Western's distinctive copper-edged chimney and brass safety valve cover on top of the boiler, with its novel waisted form (see page 131). The overall effect is to make it look rather upright and haughty in contrast to the more streamlined locomotives that were becoming popular in the 1930s. Up to 1936, the tender transfer on the "County of Bedford" read "Great Western" flanking the company arms, but after that Hornby copied the GWR with its more modern button logo on the tender (see opposite). This logo can still be seen in the cast iron side frames of benches on some old Great Western station platforms today. The tenders for all the No. 2 Special range were also used for the No. 3 locomotives from around 1930.

THE SCARCITY VALUE OF THE SOUTHERN RAILWAY

As a Liverpool company, Hornby had a predilection for modelling the local LMS (London Midland and Scottish) locomotives and stock. The next most widely modelled was the LNER (London North Eastern Railway). Far fewer were produced in GWR (Great Western Railway) livery, and in some ranges the Southern is very rare

indeed, as few pieces were sold originally, reflecting its pedestrian reputation.

One of their rarest models is of a Southern Railway L1 Class locomotive and tender. Originally lettered A 759 – for her shed in Ashford, Kent – from 1935 she was renumbered 1759. The later version with electric mechanism is one of the hardest of all Hornby locomotives to find, as a tiny number were made by comparison with the LMS Compound No. 1185.

Dedicated Hornby collectors aim for attractive steam locomotives from the Southern Railway, perhaps as a counterpoint to the supposed stigma of running unglamorous suburban electric trains. The most glamorous locomotives running on the Southern line in the 1930s were the Schools Class, probably the finest achievement of the

designer, Richard Maunsell. Classified as 5Ps, they were supposed to be the most powerful and heavy 4–4–0s running in Europe and were particularly used for the Kent routes. They also ran on the Hastings line, which had very tight tunnel clearance, so the upper parts of the cab and tender side sheets were sharply canted inwards. The twenty locomotives in the class were all named after famous public schools, from No. 900 "Eton" and No. 901 "Winchester" through to No. 919 "Harrow".

The lack of modern 4–4–0s and the fact that the "Bramham Moor" could easily pass for a Schools were probably what prompted Hornby to model the class as its one and only No. 4 locomotive in 1937, rather than any

above: A 1937 GWR "Caerphilly Castle", one of the Hornby Series No. 3 locomotives, showing the later button logo on the tender.

below: *The 1936 LMS "Royal Scot" with smoke deflectors, another of the stalwart Hornby Series No. 3 Locomotives.*

far right: *The No. 2 Special Tank Locomotives were the workhorses of the Hornby Series; this GWR version from 1936, with late button logo, is in unusually good condition.*

right: *Unlike Märklin, Hornby often did not go into great detail to make export models fit their markets. This very rare 1937 "Princess Elizabeth" is in western Argentinian livery.*

left: *The little 1928 DC electric No. 1 Tank Locomotive was beautifully enamelled and still kept a toy-like quality, with small wheels and large brass brush caps.*

desire to promote the Southern Railway. The "Eton" (see below) was a very acceptable replica of the prototype. It has the compact and taut lines of the engine, but compromises with its use of the standard No. 2 special tender which omits the distinctive "tumble-home" on the upper side sheets. It was very popular at the time, despite being both an SR locomotive and more expensive than the No. 2 Specials. It remains one of the most sought-after locomotives. Although rarer in clockwork, the 20-volt version is more collectible.

below: *The Southern Railway Schools Class had an air of compact power about them, well captured in the 1937 Hornby "Eton" model.*

COLLECTORS' PITFALLS

There are many pitfalls for the unwary in collecting old Hornby trains. Most are caused by the unscrupulous or concealed restoration of paintwork and the replacement of components. However, Hornby inadvertently laid up trouble for the future by selling locomotives and tenders separately, probably to keep the apparent price down; it is not uncommon to find locomotives in the same company liveries sold at the time with the wrong tenders. In 1939, Hornby started finishing locomotives and tenders in a matt lacquer, which means that locomotive and matching

tender could have quite legitimately come in non-matching finishes.

A more serious problem concerns the use of alloy in Hornby locomotives. Until 1934 Hornby used lead for the cast components in its 0 Gauge and Dinky Toy ranges. As the Dinky Toy range grew, Hornby copied the diecasting technology of the Dowst Company in the USA. Using Kipp machines, a molten magnesium-zinc alloy – mazac – was injected into moulds under pressure. On the positive side, it enabled very light, cheap and accurate castings to be made. On the negative side, the alloy was very sensitive to contamination by minute quantities of lead. The decay of mazac is usually known as "metal fatigue" and affects Hornby 0 Gauge, Hornby-Dublo and Dinky Toys from the 1930s and Märklin, Trix and some smaller British diecast toy manufacturers into the early 1950s. Metal fatigue causes the alloy to expand, distort, crack and blister, as well as becoming brittle and fragile. Unfortunately, although Meccano designers were aware of this problem at the time, they did not yet know how to cure it, other than by suggesting coating the fatigued areas with varnish.

Metal fatigue can badly affect the driving and bogie wheels of some of the finest Hornby 0 Gauge locomo-

tives, as well as Mansell coach wheels and wagon wheels. When inspecting a locomotive that has lain in its box untouched for many years, it is extremely important to remove all loose fragments of fatigued alloy that could damage paintwork.

"PRINCESS ELIZABETH"

Sadly, Frank Hornby died in 1936, so he never saw his company's largest locomotive, the "Princess Elizabeth", which was produced in 1937 under the auspices of his son, Roland. The original LMS 4–6–2 Pacific "Princess Elizabeth" was constructed at Crewe in 1933, to a design by Sir William Stanier. She was one of the first Pacifics on the LMS and worked the Euston–Glasgow route with great success, setting a world non-stop average speed record in November 1936.

Stanier had been apprenticed at the GWR Swindon works and brought many Great Western features with him to the LMS, most notably the distinctive taper boiler that improved steam output. This was well represented in the model, which broke new ground for Hornby. Its most important feature was a six-coupled 20-volt mechanism, which enabled their production of a 4–6–2 locomotive for the first – and only – time. It followed remarkably well the lines of the prototype locomotive and tender, and included abundant detail that would thrill the older boy who was the target market for this piece. It came in a velvet-lined wooden box, covered in either red or dark blue rexine, with an illustration of the locomotive on the inside of the lid. Nevertheless, critics did carp about the hump-backed firebox and the complete lack of outer hanging frame for the rear pony, both of which could easily have been avoided.

Around 7,000 examples were made between 1937

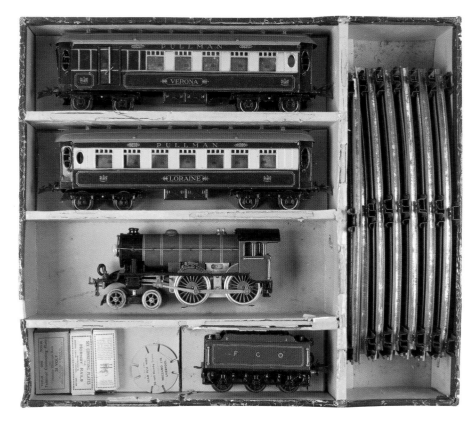

and 1940, but a high proportion appear to have survived because of a combination of factors: their initial expense, the fact that they came in protective wooden cases, and the fact that their owners were usually older boys. Paradoxically, another reason was the dreaded metal fatigue. Taking advantage of the ability to produce accurate and detailed mazac castings, Hornby used them all over the locomotive and tender – all the wheels, buffers, cross-heads, cab backhead, tender coal chute and axle boxes – and all can crack, blister or crumble to dust. Because metal fatigue could occur shortly after purchase, many "Lizzies" were seldom played with, especially after toy production ceased in 1941 and it

above: *This No. 3 Pullman Set c. 1937, is all the more collectible because it is in the livery of the western Argentinian railway.*

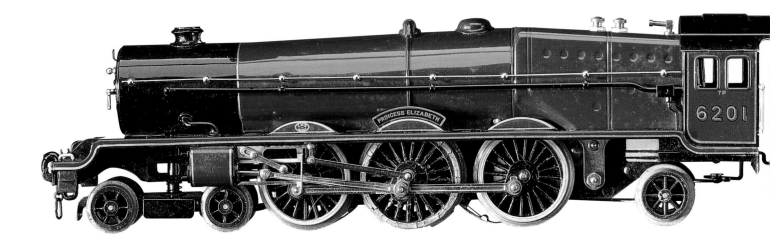

was no longer possible to expand sets or to get replacement parts.

The final reason was less obvious. The locomotive was an anomaly in the range in 1937. Although it had been designed to run happily around a 60cm (2ft) radius tinplate track, its huge length made it look ridiculous in comparison. To counter this problem, in 1937 Hornby introduced a range of much heavier drawn, solid steel rail with a 98cm (38.5in) radius, and also brought out half curves, straights, half and quarter straights, left and right hand points and buffer stops.

above: The 1937 LMS version of Hornby's only Pacific, the "Princess Elizabeth", displays its rather ungainly firebox profile and lack of frame around the pony wheels.

This new track allowed the fast and smooth running of the large locomotive, heading a rake of No. 2 LMS corridor coaches. It bears a startling similarity to the contemporary "Modellschienen" (model track), which had been produced for Märklin's admirable range of eight-coupled locomotives. Despite its visual appeal, however, the steel track had only a short production run at Hornby, and its cost militated against its success – in 1938–9 even a fairly simple rectangular layout with two running lines and four

short sidings would have cost more than double the price of the locomotive.

Because the pre-war "Princess Elizabeth" is an oddity, and was unlikely to have continued in production even if the war had not broken out, many collectors do not wish to own one. However, those who do buy one have to be very careful about the quality of any that they find. The LMS lake livery is very prone to fading (see page 124), and an example in a flat chocolate finish, even if it is unchipped, is worth considerably less than one that is still a rich, glossy maroon. The plush lining of the wooden presentation case may have looked very impressive when new, but it can retain damp and cause paint damage to the offside of a locomotive that looks fine from the nearside. The cases themselves are sturdy, but the rexine finish can peel quite badly and the cases can also retain inside all the broken mazac fragments that can rattle around and gouge paintwork.

The tinplate-bodied Hornby 0 Gauge "Princess Elizabeth" should never be confused with the non-scale-length plastic-bodied 00 Gauge "Princess Elizabeth", which was first produced by Rovex in 1950, and then by

Tri-ang, Tri-ang-Hornby and Hornby Railways up to 1974. It was very popular and tens of thousands were manufactured, but it is of very small value compared to its larger sister.

FREIGHT STOCK

The Hornby primary range of four-wheel freight stock went through three main phases of development: 1920–23, with a solid base that was plain and very toy-like; 1923–30, when the lighter and more spindly open axle-guard base was used (see page 120); and 1930 onwards, with the introduction of the standard base,

which was plainer and stronger, with more realistic detailing of springs and axleguards (see page 134). From 1931, the old-fashioned drop-link coupling was replaced by the new automatic coupling, which linked stock much more easily. The cheap M range of wagons was lighter and plainer, with simplified hook couplings, and is not very collectible.

Assuming they are in good condition, certain types of four-wheel wagons will always be popular with collectors, whatever their period of manufacture. These include private owner vans, gunpowder vans, tank wagons, snow ploughs as well as the No. 0 series of lithographed vans. Later private owner vans manufactured by Hornby (see page 120 for the earlier types) included "Cadbury's Chocolate" (1932–1942) and, the last in the series, "Palethorpe's Sausages" (1938–42). The gunpowder vans for each railway company were finished in red – a traditional warning colour – except for the Great Western version, which was finished in grey after 1928.

The more common petrol and oil tank wagons, such as "Shell" and "Pratt's", can be found relatively cheaply in

below: *The GWR brass safety valve cover looks incongruous on the rare "County of Bedford" in central Argentinian livery.*

good condition even now, while "Esso" and "Power Ethyl" had shorter production runs, so are rarer. Others include "National Benzole", "Redline Glico", "Castrol", "Mobil" and "BP". One of the more difficult fuel-tank wagons to find is the "Pool", produced between 1940 and 1942 and again for a short period between 1946 and 1948. Finished in grey, it represented the prototype that carried "pooled" fuel from all the petrol companies during World War II.

Two of the most desirable tank wagons carried products that could not have been more dissimilar: milk and

bitumen. Both launched in 1928, the two wagons were almost identical in construction and retailed at more than twice the price of the fuel wagons. In return for the extra expenditure, the buyer obtained a wagon that was much more detailed, with a tank of larger diameter fitted with securing beams at each end, braced by wire stays. The milk wagons (see page 137) were fitted with access ladders to the filler and tank valves, which justified the extra cost. The tank of the milk wagon was painted in cream and carried the United Dairies logo, while the tank of the bitumen wagon was blue and bore the Colas logo. In 1936, the milk logo was changed to Nestlé's Milk and the Colas tank was now painted in red. Examples of these wagons in good condition are so scarce that a rake of either would be an unattainable dream for even the most avid of Hornby collectors.

The range of four-wheel wagons produced by Hornby was extensive. There are some rare variations, such as the pink SR No. 1 Refrigerator Van and the green SR Gas Cylinder, which are highly desirable and expensive. However, most of these wagons are not particularly valuable and represent the affordable core of many running collections: brake vans, fibre wagons, open wagons, crane trucks, luggage vans, cattle trucks, barrel wagons and hopper wagons are typical. But whatever the rakes of Hornby freight stock consist of, they sound absolutely wonderful as they wobble, rattle and clatter around the track and over points.

Bogie (eight-wheel) stock was an early introduction to the Hornby range. In 1922 the No. 2 Timber Wagon was issued, which comprised a flat bed with ten metal stakes holding a load of planed timber. The rest of the No. 2 vehicles followed: the Lumber Wagon carrying logs, the Trolley or Well Wagon with or without cable drums, the Cattle Truck, the Breakdown Van and Crane, and the Luggage Van. Although all these bogies are quite simple models, their size and bulk gave added realism to many enthusiasts' layouts.

In 1936, a realistic set of freight stock was added to the range: the three high-capacity wagons. Although two pressings were identical and the third similar, Hornby lithographed each one differently for three railway companies. The NE version was a timber-bodied Fletton brick wagon, while the GW and LMS versions both represented the new type of steel-bodied wagons for carrying locomotive coal. Hornby further added to the realism by providing the wagons with miniature brick and coal loads as accessories.

PASSENGER STOCK

Like freight stock, Hornby passenger stock divides into the interesting and the ordinary, with most of the four-wheel stock falling into the latter category. Honourable exceptions include the very first No. 1 Passenger Coaches, produced between 1921 and 1923, which were simple and toy-like, and easy to take apart, with plain roofs and brass letters on the doors. They were followed from 1924 to 1928 by thin coaches with clerestory roofs, opening doors and open axle guards; some of these can be in great demand, particularly the GWR version which had a shorter production run. The 1934 update of the No. 1 Passenger Coach more accurately represented the liveries and appearance of the modern stock of the Big Four rail companies. Unfortunately, the opening doors were lost in the process; although good-looking, they are not much in demand now. They are extremely common, as similar models remained in production until the 1960s. Hornby also produced "economy" Pullman coaches as No. 1, M1/2, No. 0 and MO models for the cheaper sets; these also look very ill proportioned and, having been produced in large quantities, remain very cheap today.

Constructional bogie coaches were introduced in 1921 with the Dining Saloon, available with the coat of arms of Pullman or of other companies that operated prior to the grouping into the Big Four: London North West, Great Northern, Midland and Caledonian. Although they are quite toy-like in appearance, they were in fact of heavy and complex construction, with each window frame and step, for example, a separately applied part. They are rarely found today in good condition. The later versions, revised as the non-constructional

opposite: Delights in the 1939–40 **Hornby Book of Trains** *included the clockwork Goods Train Set and the Passenger Train Set.*

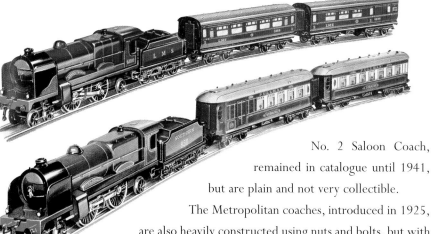

No. 2 Saloon Coach, remained in catalogue until 1941, but are plain and not very collectible.

The Metropolitan coaches, introduced in 1925, are also heavily constructed using nuts and bolts, but with sides of lithographed rather than painted sheet. Because of the limited range of bogie coaches, Hornby customers were advised to use them as LNER passenger coaches. Few survive in good condition, but look convincing when they do. They are reasonably long, with punched-out windows and celluloid glazing, and some versions were available with interior lighting. Two types of coaches were made: a full 1st and a 3rd composite, both with non-corridor compartments.

The "Riviera Blue" bogie coaches, introduced in 1926 with the Nord 4–4–2, were convincing representations of Wagons-Lits dining and sleeping cars. The techniques

employed in their manufacture informed the later No. 2 Special Pullman Coaches. The painted blue finish is very fragile, particularly on the 1920s versions, so they are rare in good condition (see page 121).

The No. 2 Pullman used the same pressings as the saloon coach, but was finished in a more attractive brown and cream livery, with "Pullman" under the windows. The No.2 Special Pullman, introduced in 1928 (see left and page 129) was Hornby's most expensive coach, over five times the price of a four-wheel No. 1 Pullman. The completely new and elaborate body manages to convey bulk and grandeur, despite not being an accurate scale length. The roof had a raised centre section fitted with cast ventilators, flat roof-walking plates at each end and clips for destination boards at the edges near the gutter rails. The body detail included opening vestibule doors set back at each corner, with oval windows, oval lavatory windows, celluloid window strip printed with interior detail, battery boxes and, until 1931, compensating bogies with white-tyred Mansell wheels. There can be few greater Hornby pleasures than lifting off the lid of a sturdy dark pink box for the first time to reveal a gleaming No. 2 Special Pullman with richly coloured paintwork. If kept dry and in the dark, these coaches can look as good today

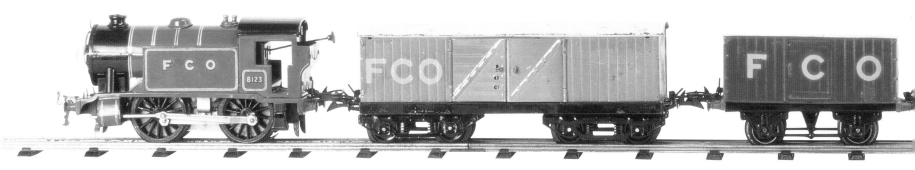

as they did when new, which is a tribute to the quality of their original construction.

Unlike the No. 2, which was simply named "Pullman", the Specials had individual names: "Loraine", "Zenobia" and "Grosvenor". The composite versions differed in having opening double doors at one end for luggage and were named "Verona", "Alberta" and "Montana". All were originally issued with cream roofs, but these were changed to grey in 1930. On the Riviera Blue pressing was based the red-painted No. 3 Mitropa Dining Car and Sleeping Car, which, although they were made between 1931 and 1941, are now extremely rare; most examples found today are replicas.

The most successful and commonly sought after Hornby coaches are the No. 2 lithographed Passenger and Corridor series. The Passenger Coaches of suburban compartment outline were introduced in 1935, followed by the mainline Corridor Coaches in 1937, to complement the No. 2 Special and No. 3 locomotives. Within the constraints of the 60cm (24in) track radius, Hornby made the coaches as scale-length as possible; they look fine headed by a 4–4–0, but less so behind the "Princess Elizabeth" or when compared with an Exley equivalent (see page 170). It would be a pleasing pipe dream to imagine the proper scale-length coach that Hornby might have made in the 1940s if war had not intervened. Nevertheless, for playthings the lithography and the detail on these coaches are of good quality and quite realistic enough.

All the No. 2 coaches use the same body pressing, but the livery of each company gives them very different characters. The LNER coaches give a very good representation of the Gresley varnished teak finish of the originals, and the GWR coaches look refined in their cream and chocolate livery with the new button logo. All the corridor coaches had destination-board clips and were designed to take accessory flexible fabric concertina corridor connectors. At half the price of the No. 2 Special Pullmans, they were originally good value and have proved fairly durable, but can be prone to scratching, as the sides are sheer, with no details in relief. As with all Hornby lithographed pieces, the glazing is simply clear lacquer coated over bare tinplate, so these areas are vulnerable to spotting, discoloration or even corrosion. Even if the rest of the coach appears perfect, damage to these areas can considerably reduce market value.

opposite: *Famous names: "The Royal Scot" and "The Golden Arrow" both featured in the 1939–40* **Hornby Book of Trains.**

below: *This 1930s Hornby export freight train for the western Argentinian railway is a rare survivor.*

A COMPLETE MODEL RAILWAY

Locomotives and rolling stock are really just the bare bones of a toy railway layout; the essential pleasure is the use of the imagination. Almost from the beginning, Hornby wanted to give children a helping hand with their dreams and produced a wide range of additional features. Laid out together, the pieces look magnificent, particularly in the dark with the electrical accessories all lit up and a locomotive tearing around the track with headlamp blazing.

Stations

A station is the most important start of a complete layout. Hornby's first station, Windsor, was introduced in 1923. It was a good representation of a brick-built suburban station with two platform ramps and featured clips in the base for candle lighting – from 1932 it had electric lighting in the form of decorative lamp brackets. In 1928, when a simpler No. 1 version was introduced, it became known as the No. 2 Station. The platform colour changed from grey to green and the doors on to the platform actually opened. The No. 2E stations are more desirable, but very often the lamp brackets have broken; these are surprisingly difficult and costly to replace.

In 1936 the choice of stations expanded: Wembley, Ripon, Reading, Margate and Bristol. Bristol was only in production briefly and is the rarest. The same basic pressing was used for the 1937 No. 4 station, but the lithography was updated and it

featured an open access to the booking hall instead of an illustration, and a cast ticket-office barrier.

Substantial termini or through stations could be built up with the addition of island platforms, available in electric and non-electric versions, and passenger platforms. There was also a No. 2 goods platform, which evolved from a simple canopy to a proper building in 1928. It had two sliding doors and windows each side under a slate roof, and the goods crane at one end was a bonus not included in the cheaper version.

1 By 1926 the candleholders of the Windsor Station were gone and the front of the platform had sockets for making a terminus with the ramps.

2 This Hornby country scene includes such rarities as the Countryside Sections, the early Footbridge, the "Colman's Mustard" Van, and Milk and Bitumen Tank Wagons.

Tunnels and bridges

Tunnels were all simply made of wood and card, covered with a type of flock to imitate green sludge with sandy outcrops. The tunnel commonly known as the Tinprinted Tunnel is the most popular with collectors; it incorporates two brick portals with canted side walls and the landscape in between is lithographed and embossed in a realistic and complex manner. Even rarer is the pair of tinprinted tunnel portals, designed for adding to home-made mountains.

Footbridges were usually very plain, with the exception of the lattice girder footbridge, an unwieldy piece with bent-metal supporting walls painted to simulate brick, wooden posts and tinplate steps and deck. It is very rare in any paint variation and in good condition fetches large sums.

Dressing the landscape

Probably the most eccentric accessories ever produced by Hornby were the Countryside Sections. They are very close in style to the town and green sections made by Lionel in the USA at around the same period. They comprised fifteen different pieces of card, each of differing size and shape, laid out with fields, gates, roads and

painted loofah hedges. Put together, they made a very comprehensive and pleasing landscape. They were only made from 1932 to 1934 and are extremely rare, so few collectors are lucky enough to have many pieces.

Loofah hedges on wooden bases were also sold by the dozen, as were loofah oak and poplar trees with thin wooden dowel trunks. These trees are scarce today as their circular diecast stands suffer from metal fatigue.

Other set dressings included telegraph poles (once familiar sights on Britain's railways, festooned with wires linking signal boxes), loading gauges (used for ensuring safe clearance around locomotives and rolling stock), platelayer's huts to shelter the hard-working permanent waymen, electric and non-electric lamp standards, and diecast hoardings with a wide range of advertising posters.

BUILDINGS AND ACCESSORIES

Although they were not nearly as extensive or elaborate as the Märklin range from the same period, Hornby buildings and accessories had a lightness and charm that was lacking in the more serious and sturdy German pieces. They were also made to a more consistent and accurate scale. Whereas a tireless Märklin station porter might be confronted by a newspaper trolley that towered over him, his Hornby opposite number only had to face at worst a slightly oversized milk churn or tinplate trunk. The range of accessories was at its peak in around 1934 and, interestingly, prices dropped considerably between 1928 and 1938, as the Depression squeezed demand.

The engine sheds copy a type of brick-built shed commonly found at the time and look magnificent on any layout. Their design is restrained, but richly coloured and full of realistic detail, even down to the representation of shadows cast by the gutter downpipes. The most expensive shed, the hefty No. E2E (see page 140), cost more in the mid-1930s than a complete clockwork goods train set and, unlike some pieces, its price had climbed rather than fallen by 1938. The No. E1E shed was half the size, while the No. 1 and No. 2 sheds were the same size but with clockwork track and no electric light; No. 1A and 2A sheds were similar, but shorn of detail and cheaper. The only major production change, in 1935, was to replace the simulated planking on the inside of the doors with a plain green finish. Like the bulk of tinprinting work for Hornby and Meccano, the engine sheds were printed by Hudson, Scott and Sons in Carlisle (see page 144).

right: *The No. 2E Signal Cabin had a hinged roof for access to a Control System lever frame, and came fitted for electric light. The rare Water Tank, once a familiar lineside landmark, was also fitted for electric light – an odd combination.*

Engine sheds are not uncommon, but seldom found in pristine condition. The angled roof lights were liable to collect all the corrosive smog particles likely to fall on a typical attic layout before the 1956 Clean Air Act. Their large boxes often split or warp, but sheds with boxes usually fetch the highest price because they have often protected the contents from the elements.

Using the Control System (see page 121), signals were an integral part of a layout, even though in practice they were simply added for decoration. Hornby's Signal Cabin came out in 1924, with a cheaper No. 1 version following in 1928. It remained, little changed, in Hornby's catalogue until 1957, making it one of the longest-running buildings. The signal was connected by rod to a counter-balanced lever at the base of the post and was available with single or double arms, junctions with two separate posts or as a gantry that spanned the track; the electrically lit version is extremely sought after. Although it is rather over scale, this series of signals is one of the finest efforts to recapture the feel of British semaphore signals by any of the tinplate manufacturers.

Level crossings were surprisingly elaborate and decorative. The most expensive, the No. E2E, had double gates fitted with electric lamps and twin track. Original models, introduced in 1924, can be identified by the "Beware of the Trains" notices and the more detailed tinprinting of the road and verges.

Part of the pleasure of collecting Hornby products is the way that they fall into distinct series, each with their own character. Of the nine accessories sets, the first three, introduced in 1924, are the most interesting, with the greatest number of paint and lithography variations. The early issues came in stylish pale card boxes with pictorial lids and "Hornby Series" transfer in one corner;

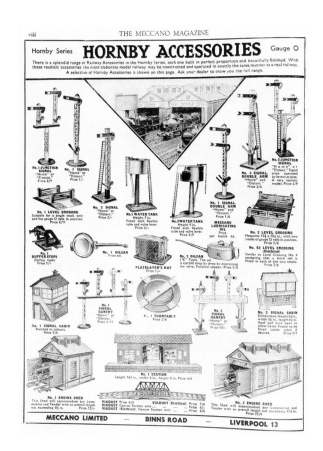

later ones fell in line with the rest of the range, with mottled purple boxes and more colourful labels.

No. 1 consisted of a sack truck with two trunks, hamper and suitcase – the sort of bulky luggage that it is now all but extinct in real life, as are the porters who used to struggle with it. For the first two years the hamper bore a Carlisle label, after the home town of the lithographers, before it was dropped in favour of the more cosmopolitan London. Early Carlisle hampers are highly coveted.

No. 2 was a set of six milk churns and truck. and No. 3 two painted tinplate benches and neatly lithographed

above: *A page from* **The Meccano Magazine.** *Today the K-type oil can is particularly sought after.*

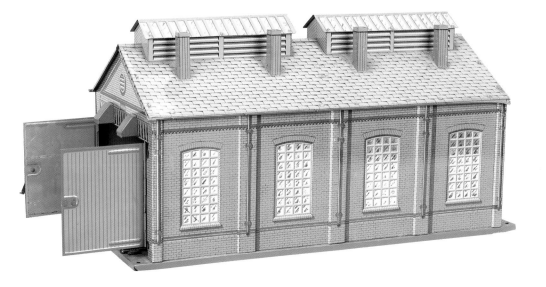

nametape and platform ticket machines and postbox. The benches are particularly fragile and often seem to suffer from bent or missing legs.

Of the six other sets, the No. 7 (watchman's hut, brazier, shovel and poker) is probably the most entertaining – there is even a small tab on the hut to hang up the shovel. A complete boxed example is a particular find, as the poker is usually missing.

above left: *The 1931 advertisement for Hall's Distemper fits in well to a Hornby layout, but is actually a rare and oversized Dinky Toy.*

above right: *Probably the largest and finest piece of lithographed tinplate made in Britain, the 1935 No. 2 Engine Shed is hard to find without rust or dirt damage.*

Hornby produced the minutiae of railway life, from a shunter's pole to a variety of keys, to the same high standards as the rest of the range. A pleasing discovery would be a copper No. 2 oil can (K Type), made for Hornby by Kaye's, manufacturers of the full-size articles. Today, one in its original red box would cost as much as a good locomotive.

Collectors – and auctioneers – often get the greatest satisfaction from finding "fresh" collections; these may have been assembled long ago by pioneer enthusiasts, but usually refer to family train sets found in attics or cellars. Such discoveries are a little like archaeological digs – each collection is unique and reflects the tastes and personality of the original owner. Of course the most valuable pieces are usually the locomotives and rolling stock, but the rare small accessories and oddities give character and breadth to a collection.

MODELLED MINIATURES AND THE DINKY TOY RANGE

From small beginnings, great ideas spring. In 1931, Hornby introduced the Modelled Miniatures, to fit alongside the railway accessories. The original range of lead railway figures and miniature push-along train sets was extended in 1933 to include the 22 Series of colourfully painted lead vehicles. Intended simply to complement Hornby 0 Gauge locomotives and stock, the range grew rapidly and in April 1934 was given the now-legendary Dinky Toy name. Its popularity soon eclipsed the Hornby parent to became the mainstay of Meccano.

The figures in all these sets were well detailed and painted; after 1938, they were reissued in a smaller size, in plain boxes with illustrated inserts. Most of the figures were "dressing" for railway platforms – station staff and passengers and such vanished breeds as the greaser and the Pullman car waiter. The hat box carried by the hotel porter bears the initials "FH" for Frank Hornby. Exiled to the rustic byways of the layout would be the farmyard animals (set No. 2) and the shepherd and his flock from set No. 6. Ironically, this, the cheapest of them all, is now the scarcest and most valuable. It is often worth checking through mixed groups of Britains and Johillco farm animals for ones marked "Hornby Series" on the underside.

The last set, No. 13, was Hall's Distemper Advertisement (see opposite). As an early Dinky Toy, it is sought after in mint and boxed condition; unsurprisingly, the advertising board is almost always a replica.

FOREIGN FIELDS

From the very earliest days, in 1920, Hornby sold rolling stock specially lettered for the French market and opened first an office and then, in 1921, a factory in France. From 1923, locomotives were exported back to Britain in the pre-nationalization liveries of Nord, Etat and PLM. As sales continued to grow, so more production was transferred to France, with a new plant opening at Bobigny in the early 1930s. French Hornby's success continued throughout the 1930s and it developed a range that sometimes surpassed the home factory in inventive design.

Hornby's move into America was less illustrious. The market was already crowded with similarly priced railways and Hornby did not have the backing to succeed. After considerable litigation to protect his patents, Hornby opened a factory at Elizabeth, New Jersey – not far from the Lionel factory – to make Meccano sets. In 1927 he launched two locally built passenger sets; although they were adapted with bell, lamp and cowcatcher to look American, they still resembled the humble M1 0–4–0 and did not live up to expectations. The American-outline four-wheel Pullmans, boxcar, tank car and caboose were more pleasing, but the factory closed in 1930. Unsold stock went to Canada and then to Britain, where the lettering was changed and

below: *This western Argentinian version of the famous 1937 Southern Railway Schools Class "Eton" is both elegant and very rare.*

above: *Another part of a Hornby collection from Argentina: this clockwork "Yorkshire" is in western Argentinian livery.*

automatic couplings fitted. Original American-built pieces are now quite difficult to find; the simplest way to tell them from the British versions that were made later is by their T-couplings.

Even now, enthusiasts make regular discoveries of extremely rare locomotives and stock in special export liveries for countries such as Sweden, Denmark, New Zealand and Canada. More conventionally, material was produced for Switzerland, but the largest export markets for special liveries were South Africa and especially Argentina, where the British had built the railway system. Locomotives and stock were sold in Argentina between 1922 and 1940. They usually appear as FCO (western Argentina), FCCA (central Argentina) and FCS (southern Argentina), with black freight liveries that were not used elsewhere. The remarkable black FCO "Princess Elizabeth" (see page 126) makes the green FCO "Yorkshire" above look quite conventional, and it is unlikely that even serious collectors will see more than a handful of black FCO "Etons" (see page 141) in their lives.

HORNBY-DUBLO

Trix and Märklin both introduced 00 Gauge AC three-rail electric railway systems in 1935. The Märklin range for the British market range was small, but the successful Trix range (see page 110) was more of a threat to Hornby, so in 1937 Hornby started working on their own range.

Hornby-Dublo, introduced in 1938, broke new ground in several ways. Although it was a three-rail electric system, like its rivals it operated on direct, not alternating, current. In our world of standardized electricity supply, it is hard to conceive of homes receiving power from various private companies, some AC, some DC, and in a variety of voltages. Hornby was also aware that many customers would have no electricity at all, so the 12-volt DC system would work well with an accumulator.

Under the guidance of Ronald Wyborn, Meccano's long-serving chief electrical engineer, an efficient permanent magnet was developed, known as the horseshoe type after its shape. With a permanent field, there was no need to mechanically reverse polarity for direction change; the new locomotives could draw away smoothly when the control was turned clockwise from centre, slowing as it was moved back, and reversing as it went anti-clockwise. The motor was fitted with vertical armature, driving the wheels via a worm gear.

Hornby started with a clean sheet when designing the Dublo track; nevertheless it bears a startling similarity to Märklin track of the period. It is lighter and thinner than the German version, but also has cream-coloured ballast and sleepers printed on folded tinplate. Quite complex layouts could be made up using manual points, small joining sections and large radius curves. For the dedicated enthusiast, pre-war track has an appeal as the colouring is mellower, and the outer rails are either brass or plated brass. It is always identifiable by the Hornby-Dublo label between the rails; after the war, the label was on the side of the track. Although pre-war track is not generally sought after by collectors, the two-rail clockwork track is now very scarce and liked by some, as it looks more realistic than three-rail track.

After the introduction of hot metal injection diecasting in 1934, Meccano considerably increased its skill in mould design. The first diecast Dinky Toys were fairly simple, but by 1938 the new models were accurate replicas of actual vehicles. These skills were turned to the production of cheap, lightweight components for the Dublo locomotives. At a stroke, Hornby had created the finest small-gauge toy railway of its day, with accurately represented outlines of current British locomotives.

A4 AND N2 LOCOMOTIVES

The most celebrated pre-war Hornby-Dublo Gresley locomotive is described on pages 106–107. The other was the N2. These snub-nosed little 0–6–2 tank locomotives were an equally brilliant design. They were

first built in 1920–21, primarily for the suburban lines out of King's Cross. They had internal cylinders, superheated high-set boilers and short chimneys which gave them a squat, powerful appearance.

This maid of all work fulfilled the same role on Hornby-Dublo lines; it is far and away their most common locomotive. Over sixty different versions were produced from October 1938 until production stopped, under G & R Wrenn, in 1993. Even the pre-war electric EDL7 with the weaker horse-shoe motor was an excellent load hauler. The action of the coupling rod driving the wheels together without visible valve gear looks very powerful (see page 145).

The casting of the N2 body is impressive, from the complex, crisp detailing down to the tiny "Hornby" raised at the top of the smokebox door. Unfortunately, this attention to detail was then let down by a characteristic Hornby economy measure. As with the 0 Gauge range, Hornby wanted to get the maximum sales around the country out of one design. So, apart from the correct

below: *The EDP1 Passenger and the EDG7 Tank Goods sets were popular items in the 1939–40* **Hornby Book of Trains.**

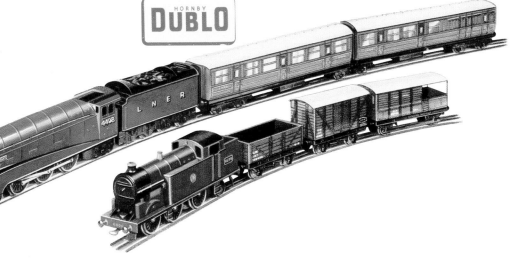

black LNER freight livery, they issued spurious models in the liveries of the other Big Four companies: an SR version in olive green, an LMS in black and a GWR in green. Of course they look good, and the Southern and Great Western DL7 clockwork versions are particularly sought after. Sadly, the keyholes are right in the middle of the fragile gold-coloured transfers, making mint versions almost impossible to find.

The only casting variation occurs on the Great Western version, where a typical GWR brass safety-valve cover replaces the steam dome. There are also tell-tale features which appear only on pre-war examples: the lighter rear pony frame, flat tensile steel couplings and flat rather than spoon-shaped centre rail electrical pick-ups. The circular GWR button logo appeared pre-war only, apart from a brief reappearance in 1947–48. The solid disc pony wheels were painted in the same livery as the locomotive; they were made of mazac from 1938 to 1951 and from iron to 1953. Because they were interchangeable, later parts can sometimes be found on early models. If the pony wheels are spoked, they come from a British Railways period N2 from after 1953.

opposite: *The 1938 EDL7 N2 Tank Locomotive was the Hornby-Dublo maid of all work. Not many pre-war models such as this survive.*

Fortunately, metal fatigue to body shells is rarely seen now, but the protective guard irons protruding from the front and back of the chassis tend to snap off easily. The wheels on the N2s crumble in the same way as on the A4s. Boxes and wrappers for the N2s are similar to those for the A4s and all dated 9.38; they are also extremely scarce.

COACHING AND FREIGHT STOCK

Hornby-Dublo only issued three coaches before World War II. They were all LNER corridor coaches, tinprinted to represent the Gresley-designed teak finish. The first,

D1, was a conventional 1st/3rd bogie coach, but the D2 was a worthy representation of an articulated All 3rd and Brake/3rd two-coach unit of the type that plied between King's Cross and Edinburgh's Waverley Station. It had a conventional bogie at each end, with a single middle bogie that also supported a plain black metal corridor connector (see page 147).

From the Hudson, Scott and Sons archives, it is clear that as early as 1937 Meccano ordered enough components to make 50,000 articulated three-coach units. Perhaps they wondered how they were going to market or to ship such a long unit, as in September 1938 they ordered further parts to adapt the design that actually went into production. The D2 articulated coach is therefore extraordinarily rare, particularly in its original box. The bogies usually suffer from terminal metal fatigue; when found, these sets have often been sent back to the Binns Road factory for repair as early as the 1940s and returned with distinctive factory job labels on the boxes. The centre bogie only appeared in this set, so correct replacements are hard to find. As with Hornby 0 Gauge, good examples of these coaches can sparkle, but rust can easily attack the plain lacquered tinplate glazing.

If coaching stock gives elegance to a toy railway layout, then freight stock gives it character, and Hornby designers were producing some of their finest work in the late 1930s. The freight vans look and sound splendid as they rattle and sway in a long rake behind an N2 tank locomotive, evoking a bygone era.

The first vehicles – a goods van, goods brake van and open wagon (see page 146) – were released as individual items in October 1938, having appeared in the new sets the month before. Unlike the "badge-engineered" N2s, there were detail differences setting apart the stock of the

different railway companies. The most radically different were the goods brake vans. All had a common chassis, but the LMS and GWR versions had longer bodies, the LMS with duckets and double veranda ends, and the GWR with one large open end but no duckets. The LNER and SR versions had open ends and guard's duckets, and the SR van had a sandbox at each end. Old Hornby habits remained, as the order to Hudson, Scott and Sons in April 1938 ranged from 20,000 LMS bodies down to only 5,000 SR, making Southern vans rare today.

The bulk of the range – including cattle, meat and fish vans in various liveries, and horse boxes – was released in March and April of 1939, followed soon after by high-sided wagons and high-capacity wagons. Apart from a small top-up wagon order in 1940, this was the last run of freight stock before the production and sale of toys was prohibited on 1 January 1942. The high-capacity wagon was the only bogie freight vehicle issued before the war; it was a fine model of a wooden-bodied Fletton brick wagon, similar to the Hornby 0 Gauge version.

The brightest and most colourful pre-war models were the three fuel tank wagons, "Esso", "Power Ethyl"

and a paraffin supplier, "Royal Daylight". The same stock of tinprintings was used again after the war, almost certainly lasting until the models were superseded in 1953.

Boxes for freight stock were similar to the coach boxes, with useful date codes on them. Where one model appeared in different liveries, a paper sticker glued to the box end announced the identity of the company represented inside. It should be no surprise that these stickers can often be fakes, so it is worth checking carefully. Quite a number of surplus pre-war boxes were only issued after the war.

Metal fatigue has devastated much of the Hornby-Dublo freight stock produced before World War II. The most serious collectors do have good holdings, sometimes made up by cannibalizing various period vehicles. Despite the rarity of many of the pieces, prices are often low as the average enthusiast is usually scared off. The tinprinted bodies and tanks often survive in excellent condition, but are allied to a mazac chassis that looks like a roller coaster in elevation. Wheels and bogies crumble and the footsteps of the goods brake vans twist and snap; even the mazac ends of the tank wagons burst and crack.

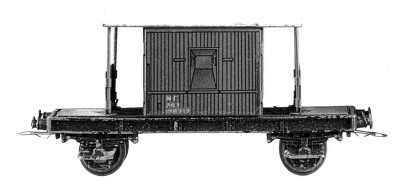

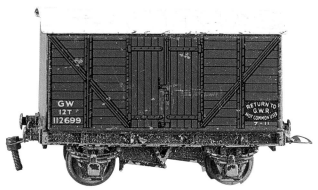

PRE-WAR HORNBY-DUBLO SETS

Pre-war Hornby-Dublo is rare enough, but entire train sets are exceptionally hard to find in fine condition. Perversely, many collectors do not actively seek out sets – possibly through lack of display and storage space – so they are sometimes not expensive in relation to the total value of the contents.

above: *Pre-war Hornby-Dublo freight stock had superb lithography, but its couplings and frames often distorted from metal fatigue.*

The LNER Passenger Train Set (DP1 clockwork or EDP1 electric) comprised the elegant "Sir Nigel Gresley" locomotive and tender, a D2 two-coach articulated unit, track, controller, a tiny spanner for removing the locomotive body and a phial of oil, which often leaks. This would have been the dream present of many a small boy wishing to emulate the record-breaking runs of the A4s on the East Coast Main Line, but it was not a cheap option. At Christmas 1939 the set cost as much as a Hornby 0 Gauge E320 "Flying Scotsman" Passenger Train Set, with extra for the transformer. And by the end of 1941, the price had doubled. This expense, in relation to the larger-gauge sets, helps to explain the relative rarity of pre-war Hornby-Dublo sets.

Page 14 of the 1939–40 *Hornby Book of Trains* was devoted to lavish details of the new EDP2 LMS Electric Express Passenger Train Set. The train was to be hauled by a superb model of the Stanier-designed non-streamlined "Duchess of Atholl", and in July 1939 Hudson, Scott and Sons in Carlisle were turning out enough tinprinted sheets to make 30,000 models of the latest LMS 1st/3rd and Brake/3rd coaches. The set would have broken new ground. The locomotive was highly detailed and accurate, with complex Walschaerts valve gear for the first time, even with sandboxes on the splashers, and, as the catalogue proudly announced, "real cut-out windows glazed with celluloid inside". Despite such preparations, only factory prototypes were produced before the war. The tinprinted coach sides were kept in storage and used for early post-war examples.

MODERN-STYLE BUILDINGS

Hornby-Dublo buildings are the most interesting and collectible pre-war accessories, but they are unusual in one respect. Having gone to the trouble of developing a highly sophisticated toy railway system, you would have expected Hornby to make them out of tinplate or mazac; in fact, they are of painted wood. Hornby was probably copying Trix Twin in Britain and Trix Express in Germany, whose first buildings were made of painted wood, but as only 1,000 boxes per component were printed, it seems likely that it was trying to reduce start-up costs.

The material of the buildings may have been old-fashioned, but the designs were absolutely up to date. They were all finished in off-cream, as if to imitate concrete, with windows and features applied as transfers. The D1 Through Station and Island Platform both have the low outline and rounded ends that followed the contemporary style of Charles Holden's work for the London Underground. Roofs were red or, occasionally, green.

These and the other buildings produced at the time – a goods depot with canopy roof, an engine shed with glazed double-pitch roof, and a small signal cabin – are rare and very hard to find with intact original boxes. Many were made of beechwood and plywood, but mahogany examples also exist, which suggests some very small production runs, almost certainly by a subcontractor. Apart from the hazards of dirt and infant graffiti, the most serious problem they are likely to suffer from is the humble woodworm.

The finest and rarest wooden building set is the D2 City Station Outfit. It originally cost almost as much as the "Sir Nigel Gresley" locomotive and tender and today far exceeds it in value. Of the large pale blue box that it came in only a few are believed to survive. Like the other buildings, the City Station (called King's Cross) was designed in the modern style. Its ingenious modular system was remarkably similar in design and ugliness to the Trix diecast Manyways station sets (see page 111). The main entrance was covered by a cantilevered awning, with a train shed the other side. This came with a curved celluloid roof and could be turned to make either a through or terminal station. With it came various platforms, ramps, removable wall panels and buffers.

If war had not intervened, useful additions to the range would have appeared in 1939 and 1940; apart from the "Duchess of Atholl", new items would have included tarpaulins, lamp standards, a viaduct and a water crane.

below: *Pre-war Hornby-Dublo sets still in their distinctive long boxes seldom survive. The bottom box contains an articulated "teak" LNER coach.*

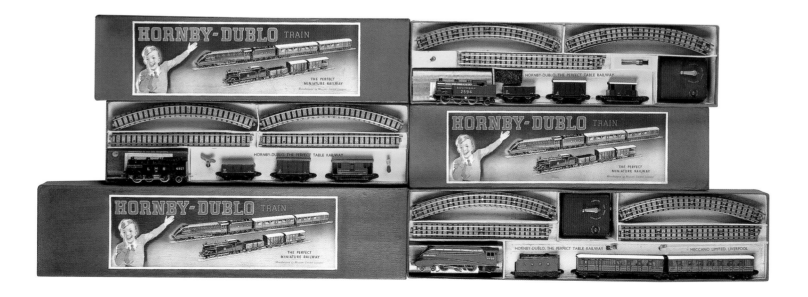

chapter 6

1945–1965

BOOM YEARS AND BEYOND

Once again world war had devastated Europe, and this time warfare had caused carnage and destruction to the civilian population. The traumas caused by the war meant that the business world was also very different. As toy-train manufacturing businesses struggled to recover, they faced bleaker prospects than in the interwar period.

MÄRKLIN

Märklin started production again in 1945 with the bare minimum of staff and machinery. With no opportunity to produce new tooling, the old pre-war model range was revived. For the first year or so, before the lithography presses worked again, much material was hand painted, probably in the workers' own homes. The very rare hand painted Mitropa dining and sleeping cars are hard to distinguish at a glance from the lithographed versions; as a key, the stamped lettering is usually crooked. Rarest of all is the TWE700 Railcar from these early post-war days (see above); although still of similar appearance to the pre-war model, it is worth three times as much.

Most of the new work at Märklin in these years was in changing production in 1947 from the unrealistic 00 Gauge, scaled at 4mm:1 foot, to the more accurate H0 Gauge, scaled at 3.5mm:1 foot. Märklin did revive parts of their 0 Gauge range, but it was to sell old stock rather than to create new models. The 1949 catalogue still showed a fine array of pieces, including the HR66 BR 01 Pacific, the CS66 Electric Locomotive, 40-cm (16-in) coaches, freight stock and buildings including Stuttgart Station. All most collectors ever see, however, are the humble R890 0–4–0 locomotive and simple four-wheel coaches; the day had passed for this type of toy train and sales ceased in 1954.

Once Märklin was back in full production, there followed a classic period up to 1952 when it designed and built some of the finest diecast and tinplate toy railways ever created. Although they were still toys, they looked far closer to scale models than playthings, despite the unrealistic three-rail tinplate track.

Märklin's most famous pre-war electric locomotive, the Swiss SBB "Krokodil", was reissued in 1947 in H0 Gauge. It is a superb model, showing clearly the inclined-bar drive; this time, it was fitted with the correct number of wheels. Production of the original CCS800 model continued with variations until 1959, but earlier examples can be easily identified by the fact that they have square rather than curved hoops over the lights (see below). Metal fatigue can still affect the bodies and chassis of these early examples, so buyers must be cautious.

Practising sensible financial husbandry, Märklin used the same castings in a variety of combinations. The motor car from the DL800, a double-ended electric locomotive in the "long bonnet" American style, was used for the ST800 Three-Unit Express Railcar, painted in a different colour scheme and with the addition of a centre passenger car and passenger trailer car, and pairing two of the trailer cars created the DT800 Railcar (see page 152). Early examples of these models in good condition are now very scarce and valuable; they are very vulnerable to chipping and are often restored.

Märklin's accessory range became very plain in the 1950s, a world away from the exuberant or majestic designs of the first thirty years of the twentieth century. The wagons, vans and tank wagons were also in appropriately drab post-war colours, but can be found with sufficient variations to engage very serious collectors. They can also suffer from serious oxidization, making mint examples hard to find and scarcer than durable pre-war tinplate stock.

Production in lithographed tinplate continued into the mid-1950s, but Märklin introduced its first plastic locomotive bodies – the rare S870 and the common CM800 – in 1953, seeing the future in that material. Plastic stock was produced to a very high standard, but held far less attraction for collectors.

Train sets such as the DA846/3 1' C 1' (1954), which contained the ubiquitous DA800 locomotive with an early plastic tender and lithographed passenger stock, were typical of the appearance of 1950s Märklin, as was the SE846/4 Passenger Set with modern electric traction from 1951. The box art of these sets is also very stylish, and pieces should be collected with their original boxes, as they can suffer badly from fine, worm-like corrosion, known as filiform corrosion, between the tinplate and the paint layer.

By 1958 the old alpha-numeric numbering system had given way to 3000 and 4000 series numbers, in time for the company's centenary in 1959. Märklin went from strength to strength, but although collectible pieces have been made after 1958, many of these are special limited

below: *Märklin's diecast H0 Gauge CCS800 version of the distinctive Swiss "Krokodil" heavy freight locomotive is a rare find. Note that this time it also has the correct number of driving wheels. Various versions were made between 1947 and 1959.*

above: *The Märklin H0 Gauge DL800, part of a series of post-war rail vehicles sharing castings.*

left: *The rather dull Hornby 0 Gauge clockwork Type 501 was still manna to post-war boys starved of new toys.*

editions, sold to adults rather than children. Today it thrives, having absorbed Trix to produce its DC range, and is now probably one of the last traditional toy and train companies still manufacturing in Europe.

HORNBY 0 GAUGE

Before 1939, Britain had vast assets in the United States, but the cost of prosecuting a war for six years meant that these assets were sold off and the country's economic heart had been mortgaged under the Lend Lease agreement. As a result, food was rationed, capital for investment was scarce and raw materials were in short supply. National industry was almost solely geared for export, in order to build up vital overseas currency reserves. The toy industry had very low priority for materials, so it was a time of desperate shortages and grimness for many British

children. The shops that had been bursting with trains before 1939 were now empty.

As with Märklin, Hornby faced shortages of staff, capital and materials. Most of the available resources went into the development of the Hornby-Dublo and Dinky Toy ranges, leaving the 0 Gauge range as the poor relation. Some No. 2 bogie and passenger stock carried on in production, as did some electric locomotives for export, but on the whole post-war buyers – if they could find anything at all – had to rely on clockwork 0–4–0 locomotives and four-wheel passenger and freight stock. In 1946, M Series pieces were revived in the No. 101 Tank Passenger Set and No. 201 Tank Goods Set. They were followed in 1948 by the more impressive No. 501 Passenger Train Set and No. 601 Goods Train Set, the latter including the rare red Shell Tank Wagon with blue rubber-stamped lettering. Although the rolling stock was still of good quality, the limitations of clockwork must have seemed galling only a generation after the 20-volt "Princess Elizabeth", and it is likely that much of this material survives in good condition because it was run very little at the time.

All models were redesigned between 1954 and 1956, and the reduction in quality is noticeable in the flimsier No. 20 and 30 sets. Rather curiously at this late stage, they were accompanied by a range of very decorative goods stock, rather in the style of the pre-war No. 0 lithographed wagons. The favourite for collectors is the Manchester Oil Refinery Tank Wagon. Sadly, the new issues could not save the 0 Gauge range, and production trickled to a halt in the early 1960s, although some pieces remained in catalogue until 1969 (see page 164 for 1950s figures). It was a sad end to a once-mighty toy railway system.

NEW DEVELOPMENTS

Hornby-Dublo had a certain amount of pre-war components left over from before the war, such as tinprinted sheets and empty boxes, but also a greatly reduced shopfloor and sales force. The drawing office immediately started making changes and improvements to the range, as a result of pre-war experiences with weak castings and metal fatigue.

Unusually, Meccano stole a march on Märklin and Trix by quickly sorting out the problem of metal fatigue, once it was recognized that as little as 1 per cent lead contamination could destroy a batch of mazac alloy. In the late 1940s, Jack Odell, one of the creators of the Matchbox range, observed that "a pennyweight of lead in a pot with two tons of metal" was enough to contaminate mazac, and he forbade its presence in his factories. The purity of mazac was now virtually ensured, although the very occasional 1950s piece does turn up with metal fatigue. Because of the relatively small number of models produced in the 1940s and small production variations, this period is very popular with collectors. They are also reassured by the lack of fatigue found in the models.

The engineers at Meccano were also very fortunate during 1946 to meet S.C. Pritchard, whose Peco company in Devon is still an important supplier of track and accessories. He had developed a new coupling, consisting of a bent vertical hook with two tails to ease coupling and uncoupling. It was used on a royalty basis and replaced the unsatisfactory pre-war coupling.

below: *The plain, post-war Hornby 0 Gauge station was a cheaper and duller shadow of its pre-war incarnation.*

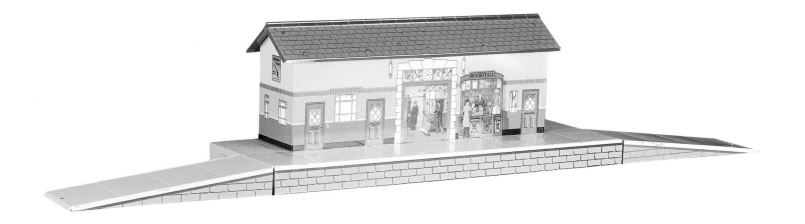

Hornby-Dublo three-rail track still had some inherent flaws. Although it proved very strong, the tinprinted base is shaped like an inverted U, and it doesn't take much pressure – perhaps from a child's foot – to make the track joints uneven, which in turn causes the rolling stock to pitch and the couplings to detach. Freight stock is particularly vulnerable, and a fine rake of stock can suddenly split and the engine and front section will go racing off. From the end of 1954 Hornby-Dublo produced their most effective metal coupling, with an extended vertical hook that solved the problem.

During the summer of 1949, the new Alnico magnet transformed the locomotive range; it was still in use in the N2 tank locomotive in 1993. It was more powerful than the horseshoe magnet and held charge better. Instead of the magnet curving around at the back of the chassis in one piece, two thicker pieces of metal cupped the armature at each side, bolted together at the back through a block magnet. For collectors today, the new magnet rendered post-war locomotives with horseshoe motors rare and desirable.

Much to the disappointment of young hopefuls, proper supplies of track did not resume until 1950, and it is noticeable that there are many colour variations on post-war track, suggesting repeat orders from various sources. (Tony McMillan, a long-standing Meccano manager, has revealed that the press tools to make the track were manufactured at Thomas Keatings' in Billingshurst in West Sussex in around 1947.) Track now had the "Hornby-Dublo" name on the side of the ballast, rather than between the rails. Over the years, useful additions included isolating rails for independent control of track sections, electric and manual uncoupling rails, roadway section for level crossings and crossover. For someone building up a running layout today, finding a good terminal rail for connection to the controller is vital as the solder joints underneath often come apart.

In general, British toy railways have less play value than the American equivalents, which were packed with an infinite supply of furiously buzzing and clattering electrical accessories. One of the few Hornby-Dublo items that comes close is the five-road turntable, launched in 1956. Although it was not motorized, like its Märklin equivalent, it allowed locomotives to be turned smoothly and it ingeniously created more space for storage on compact layouts.

AT LAST, THE NEW TRAINS

The first new train set for the home market – the EDG7 tank goods train sets in LMS, LNER, GWR and SR liveries – finally left the Binns Road factory in late 1947. Very small numbers were issued and no individual pieces were yet available. All the N2 0–6–2 tank locomotives had features beloved of Hornby-Dublo enthusiasts, such as gold maker's label and large circular spectacle windows at the back of the cab. These early passenger sets, with the old-fashioned horseshoe motor, are now rare in good condition. Quite apart from lack of supply, they were also, in an era of low wages and very high taxation for the wealthy, very expensive: the 1948 EDP1 "Sir Nigel Gresley" cost more than twice what it had nine years earlier. They are reasonably popular with collectors, provided that they are not faded, which is often the case with the LMS lake livery (see page 124).

Despite the promised arrival of new express locomotives in early 1948, none appeared until May, when the LMS non-streamlined Pacific "Duchess of Atholl" was at last available to the express-starved public, nine years later than planned and eleven years after the original locomotive was built.

When individual locomotives went on sale again in British toyshops, from June 1948, minor differences were detectable: the first "Sir Nigel Gresley" locomotive was similar to the pre-war model (see page 147), although it had cut-away skirts over the wheels and detailed Walschaerts valve gear; the GWR "button" logo was briefly reused before being replaced by "GWR" in serifed capital letters (see below) and the LNER locomotive was now available in green as well as black. The locomotives soon acquired the new Alnico motor and various parts were improved and strengthened.

A notable and valuable rarity is a "Duchess of Atholl" from a short run issued in 1951, with the lettering and border to the nameplate finished in yellow (see below left). One of the rarest of all Hornby-Dublo locomotives actually appeared in the mid-1950s, after production had officially finished. Some people who sent their "Duchess of Atholl" locomotives back to Binns Road for repair received them back with new bodies from its successor locomotive, the BR "Duchess of Montrose"; they are distinguished by having smoke deflectors flanking the smokebox (see below right).

below: Post-war Hornby-Dublo motive power included the very rare LMS "Duchess of Atholl" with smoke deflectors, which were only issued as a factory repair item.

The attractive appearance of the N2 tank locomotives makes them popular with collectors, particularly the first GWR and SR versions (see below). Numerous small detail changes took place to liveries and castings up to 1953 when they were eventually reissued in British Railways livery. Apart from one recorded exception, all post-war N2s had a depression in the underside of the front buffer beam to allow the new heavier-gauge Peco coupling to move freely from side to side.

Because of short supply, most locomotives from this time have seen hard service, and are not very collectible unless in excellent condition or an unusual variation. One such is the Canadian Pacific locomotive issued in 1953. Hornby assumed that the Canadians would be grateful to receive a modified "Duchess" with cowcatcher and headlamp added (see opposite). They were not, and the individually boxed EDL2 Canadian Pacific Locomotive and Tender is one of the rarest Hornby-Dublo pieces known. It was accompa-

below: *The details on this early post-war Hornby-Dublo Southern Railway N2 tank locomotive are unusually well-preserved.*

nied by a black-painted caboose, based on the LMS goods brake van with brakeman's lookout added (see page 158). Only slightly less rare are the accompanying freight train and passenger train sets. They may be attractively finished in Canadian Pacific livery, but the rolling stock in both sets remains resolutely British. The marketing disaster of yesterday is the goal of the collector today.

Coaches from this period were mostly continuations of pre-war designs. The few rarities include the pre-war D2 LNER Two-Coach Articulated Unit, briefly released in 1948 for export only, and so scarce that it is worth more than the pre-war example. The new Brake/3rd and All 3rd were simply the two halves of the two-coach unit split with ordinary four-wheel bogies at each end. Rarer still is the All 3rd as it was never included in a set; it was available from 1953 with the grey roof of its British Railways successor and lingered on into 1955.

Among the freight wagons, LMS and LNER versions are usually the most common. However, the LMS Cattle Truck is rare, and, more typically, the SR Meat Van and Goods Van. They generally make attractive rakes and are popular with collectors, as they contain the essence of some of the pre-war charm without the metal fatigue problems (see page 128). Post-war tank wagons continued with the use of pre-war tinprinted tank bodies, namely "Esso", "Power Ethyl" and "Royal Daylight". Designs were adapted after 1953, so early post-war versions are popular with collectors; the green "Power Ethyl" tank displaying a hand logo is particularly sought after.

DELAYED NATIONALIZATION

After Clement Attlee's government swept a disbelieving Winston Churchill from office in 1945, it embarked on a substantial programme of nationalization that included the

health service, the coal industry, the steel industry, road transport … and, inevitably, the railways. Weakened by six years of war and severe lack of maintenance, the Big Four rail companies were in no position to resist this move and British Railways came into existence on 1 January 1948.

With a commitment to existing stock and then materials being in short supply because of the demands of the Korean War in 1951–2, Meccano could not afford to retool immediately. As a result, when collectors refer to pre-nationalization models, they are discussing ones made right up to 1953. Ironically this slow changeover was a reflection of the real world. British Railways did not emerge afresh in 1948 like a butterfly from a cocoon. It inherited a variety of running practices, decrepit equipment and a medley of rolling stock. In these days of comparative standardization, it is hard to conceive of the complexity of a 1940s mixed-owner freight train and its slow progress to its destination as it meandered from marshalling yard to marshalling yard, often shunted into a different rake on each part of the journey.

In October 1952, reflecting an improving economy

and better access to raw materials, stock in the new BR liveries at last rolled out of the Binns Road factory. Unfortunately, this surge in productivity coincided with a new range that was very dull. Although many pieces were only minor updates, the crispness and charm of the earlier models is missing; the tinprinting seems coarse by comparison and the colour schemes bland. Vast quantities of material from this period survive in poor condition and it is virtually unsaleable unless in perfect condition. However, the traditional small Hornby retail agencies were finally getting enough to sell, and earlier export drives in the USA and Canada paid off. In 1956 alone, the sister product, Dinky Toys, sold over 26 million models.

The first Hornby-Dublo locomotives in British Railways livery bore the early BR totem of a gold lion straddling a wheel. The can also be identified by their bright gloss finish, which was replaced by a more realistic matt finish in 1954. Familiar names appeared in the shops sporting new clothes: the "Sir Nigel Gresley" became the "Silver King" with a nameplate added to the smokebox,

above: *The 1953 Dublo "Canadian Pacific" should have been a great export boost, but the target audience could see the thinly disguised "Duchess" beneath and scorned it.*

HORNBY-DUBLO
32049
D1 CABOOSE
C.P.R.
GAUGE OO

PRINTED IN ENGLAND.

above: *The 1953 Canadian-market Caboose is simply an LMS Brake Van with a look-out and long stovepipe added.*

and the "Duchess of Atholl" was now the "Montrose" (see page 160). Both were finished in green, which favoured neither. The N2 tank locomotive reappeared as BR 69567, in black freight livery with spoked pony wheels, the first of numerous BR varieties of this workhorse. BR train sets first appeared in April 1953, each direct replacements for their pre-nationalization versions, such as EDP11 "Silver King" for the EDP1 "Sir Nigel Gresley".

The first completely new Hornby locomotive appeared in November 1954. It was modelled on a BR Standard 2–6–4 4MT (for mixed traffic) tank locomotive, designed in 1951 by British Railways' chief mechanical engineer, R.A. Riddles. Riddles' design was an improvement on Stanier's and Fowler's designs from LMS days (see opposite).

The Hornby-Dublo model was powerful and superbly engineered, as well as handsome. It pulled well, but suffered from a lively front pony, which could foul points. It was the first piece to be fitted with the Peco coupling with a longer vertical hook, which held together better on rough track.

Two new train sets introduced in November 1954 did have more character than most and also happen to be rare. Each was based around the Riddles EDL18 4MT tank locomotive. The EDP13 included three maroon Midland Region suburban coaches, which complement the purposeful locomotive very well, as do the bogie bolster, brick wagon and brake van in the second set, the EDG18 Tank Goods Train Set.

Another rare set briefly available from late 1956 was the EDP10. It contained the old favourite EDL7 tank locomotive with two updated Midland Region suburban coaches, now fitted with plastic windows. Its rarest feature was the long box it came in, which resembled pre-war set packaging.

BRITISH RAILWAYS COACHING AND FREIGHT STOCK

Hornby-Dublo paralleled the achievement of many car manufacturers: they took a fine design and ruined it by improvement. With an identical body, the lithography of the pretty D1 LNER teak corridor coach was replaced with the maroon and cream livery (known as "plum and spilt milk" or "blood and custard") of the BR Eastern region and was renamed D11. The LMS coach, produced in huge numbers, reappeared in the same BR livery as the D12 and is equally dull. Admittedly the All 3rd LNER teak compartment coach, turned into the maroon BR suburban coach, did look the part in a rake behind the new 4MT Standard tank locomotive.

As with the coaching stock, Hornby-Dublo reissued most of their old freight wagons in revised liveries that appeared duller and cruder than before; moreover, these wagons are rarely found in good, boxed condition and are little sought after. The old tank wagons were re-issued as "Esso" on a silver tank, "Esso Royal Daylight Paraffin" on a red tank and "Power Petrol" on a green tank – without the white hand emblem. They were soon joined by "Shell Lubricating Oil" in yellow, "Mobil" and "Mobil Oil Company Ltd" in red and "Vacuum Oil Company Limited", a division of Mobil, in the same shade of red. The "Power Petrol" label should not be confused with the earlier and more covetable pre-nationalization version.

NEW ACCESSORIES

In 1949, the most important large Hornby-Dublo building was introduced: the D1 through station. It is also the most common, often found coated with a greasy blanket of attic dust. Technically, the station was a masterpiece, constructed of light and strong aluminium, diecast by a Birmingham subcontractor; aesthetically, it was dismal. Ignoring a host of more prepossessing possibilities, the designers seem to have taken a cue from the plain Trix Manyways station (see page 111), emulating reinforced concrete, predominantly painted in a sickly shade of creamy yellow, with an orange cantilevered canopy covering the platform.

below: *The BR Standard 4MT Tank Locomotive is a good load hauler; this is the later two-rail 2218 with re-cast chimney from 1959.*

THE WINDS OF CHANGE

The early 1960s was the Macmillan era of "You've never had it so good" and the onset of capital and consumer spending after eighteen lean years. Since the introduction of the 0 gauge range in 1920, Hornby had proved repeatedly that its aim was to produce toy trains of the best quality possible for the price. A logical extension of this was to reinvent the Hornby-Dublo range almost in its entirety, using new diecastings and plastics at considerable expense. The greatest cost was incurred by phasing out three-rail track in favour of the more realistic two-rail track.

The new range took a step closer to the model-like accuracy of toy railways today. Unfortunately, the tooling costs for the new Hornby-Dublo range had a severe effect on the cash-flow of Meccano Ltd. Manufacture of a typical locomotive required over 100 separate machining operations, which meant that they could not possibly compete with Tri-ang or Playcraft, who could retail their cheaply made locomotives for half the price. The less expensive makes were inferior in many ways, but this was

above: The "Duchess of Montrose" from 1954 is simply an updated and common BR version of the "Duchess of Atholl", but she has lost some of her charm in the transition.

of little concern to the small consumer who wanted a working railway and to the parent who wanted to pay as little as possible – Meccano had read the runes incorrectly with its insistence on quality.

Meccano's Dinky Toy range continued to be successful, but Mettoy launched the competing Corgi Toy range in 1956. Packed with features and innovations, it was a serious threat to the dominance of Dinky Toys. This, combined with poor revenues from Hornby-Dublo, greatly affected profits. By 1963 the company was in severe difficulties and, with great irony, accepted the takeover offer of the makers of Tri-ang Railways, in February 1964.

Descended from the Victorian firm of G&J Lines, Tri-ang had been started in 1919 by the three Lines brothers – hence the name Tri-ang. It thrived in the 1930s with varied products ranging from Minic cars to dolls' houses and prams, turned out from a huge factory in Morden. In October 1951 the company took over Rovex, a small concern in Richmond, Surrey, that had started building plastic train sets the year before, but was under-capitalized. Lines Bros built up the mighty Tri-ang Railways range and its keen pricing and marketing success eventually forced Meccano Ltd into its arms in 1964. Although the name

Hornby continued as before, the whole range was changed and the great days of Hornby were over.

The Tri-ang–Hornby range carried on successfully until 1971, when the combined liabilities of parts of the group took Rovex–Tri-ang with it. It re-emerged as Hornby Railways and today exists profitably as simply Hornby, turning out the finest 00 Gauge models it has ever made, sourced from China.

FAREWELL TO STEAM

The first new-generation Hornby-Dublo three-rail locomotive was the Western Region "Bristol Castle", released in October 1957. Although the original was an example of Collett's powerful and compact design for GWR, she was actually built in July 1948, after nationalization. When King George VI died suddenly in February 1952, she replaced her sister locomotive "Windsor Castle", which was in shop at the time, and headed the royal funeral train. "Bristol Castle" then retained her new identity until she was sadly scrapped in February 1965; like so many locomotives, she was at the height of her powers.

Hornby's "Bristol Castle" was built only thirty years after the 0 Gauge "Caerphilly Castle", but is in every way better, packed with realistic detail – even down to the tender rivets. The first version with alloy wheels was also a powerful load hauler. Later versions with nickel silver wheels looked more decorative, but tended to suffer from poor traction as the wheels were too shiny.

From 1959 onwards, virtually all locomotives appeared in two- and three-rail versions, but three-rail locomotives were produced in far smaller quantities and are now much rarer. Older models were reworked into new, but short-lived, guises. The "Silver King" reappeared as "Mallard", at last commemorating Gresley's world record-breaking A4, updated with a double chimney, like the real locomotive. The final issue was fitted with nickel-silver wheels, making it the most sought-after post-war A4. Unfortunately it was also fitted with the black plastic bogies and pony from the two-rail "Golden Fleece", which appear ugly and inaccurate.

below: Apart from the rather shiny nickel-silver wheels and plastic tender, the 1961 "Dorchester" was one of the most attractive late Hornby-Dublo designs.

The final version of the ubiquitous N2 tank locomotive was also fitted with nickel-silver wheels, and is very sought after in three-rail form. Renumbered 3217, the body casting was revised, with a representation of coal in the bunker behind the cab and a larger safety valve. These small but crucial changes make it worth around eight times as much to a collector as the regular BR model.

above: In 1961 the three-rail "City of Liverpool" was a brand new design with plastic tender, and is considerably more sought after than the two-rail "City of London" version.

One of the most sought-after Hornby-Dublo models is the Riddles 4MT tank locomotive, which was renumbered 3218 and acquired a new running number: 80059; the discerning eye will spot that it has a re-cast chimney (see page 148). It is particularly hard to find in good condition. Both locomotives appeared in two-rail as 2217 and 2218, but are much less desirable (see page 159).

In March 1958 Hornby-Dublo released yet another new locomotive: this time it was a model of an ex-LMS 2–8–0 8F tender locomotive designed by Sir William Stanier. As with the "Bristol Castle", this is a particularly well-designed locomotive that represents neatly the plain but strong lines of the original. The small eight-coupled driving wheels tuck under the low splasher, leaving a void under the taper boiler that is well recreated in the model.

New in 1959 was a completely new "Princess Coronation" class two-rail "City of London". This was a fine model – far more detailed than the earlier "Duchesses" – but in keeping with modern demands it had a plastic tender. Its three-rail counterpart, the "City of Liverpool" (see above), is now one of the rarest Hornby-Dublo locomotives.

Hornby-Dublo's last steam locomotives were modelled on Southern Region's rebuilt West Country class Pacifics. This was a sister of the Merchant Navy class, originally designed in 1938 by the idiosyncratic Oliver Bulleid. He had wanted to produce a compact, light and streamlined locomotive, and SR restrictions led to his curious design of air-smoothed casing combined with Bulleid-Firth-Brown "box-pox" steel wheels.

It was decided in 1956 to rebuild the whole fleet with conventional external Walschaerts valve gear and shorn of

motor, one of the greatest achievements of Hornby-Dublo in 1960. This compact and powerful unit had a one-piece magnet that held charge better and enabled smoother running from low speeds. It performed record-breaking haulage feats and later went on to power the Hornby Railways range.

The very last Hornby-Dublo mainline steam locomotive was the three-rail Ringfield motor version of the "Ludlow Castle". Combining the style of its predecessors with the power of the new motor, it is justifiably the most popular of the later steam locomotives with collectors.

their air-smoothed casing. Hornby-Dublo modelled "Barnstaple" as the two-rail version of this revised class, and "Dorchester" as the three-rail one (see page 161). Although they are fine replicas, they incorporated a number of flaws, including a plastic tender and a pair of plated screw heads securing the rear of the body above the drawbar. Nevertheless, both are popular with collectors as sole examples of Hornby-Dublo mainline Southern locomotives. A key to their success was the Ringfield

BR USHERS IN DIESEL-ELECTRIC AND ELECTRIC POWER

In normal usage, the Standard locomotives British Railways was producing in the 1950s should have operated well into the 1970s and probably beyond. Unfortunately, political interference brought about the early demise of steam traction and saw some locomotives lined up in scrapyards when they were barely ten years old.

below: *The two-rail Talisman set from 1961 is attractive, but scarce in fine condition as this type of box is very fragile.*

above: Reissued pre-war 0 Gauge figures (see page 153) continued well into the 1950s, but seldom survive in fine condition. They are charming, but lack the earlier paint detail.

Since nationalization in 1948, passenger and freight charges had been set by the government; railway managers could see rapidly rising retail prices, but were unable to raise their own charges. To solve this problem the Conservative government set up the British Transport Commission, made up largely of industrialists and civil servants rather than railwaymen. Its report in January 1955, *The Modernization and Re-equipment of British Railways*, concluded that traffic should be won from roads by increased efficiency through modern traction.

By this time, even the most dedicated enthusiast had to concede that, despite their charm, steam locomotives polluted heavily and suffered from poor thermal efficiency and extended "down" time for cleaning and servicing. The British Transport Commission saw electrification as the ultimate solution, with diesel-powered locomotives as an interim measure. Plans for the production of thou-

sands of standardized locomotives were, of course, farcical, and by the early 1960s a mixed bag from different manufacturers were on the rails. In many cases, on the rails was where they stayed – the long and bitterly cold winter of 1963 produced the regular sight of steam locomotives rescuing diesel-electrics.

The railway industry went from profit in 1952 to a deficit of £86.9 million by 1961. Undeterred, in 1963 the Stedeford committee was set up, better known by the name of its most prominent member, Dr Richard Beeching. As a result of the Beeching committee's report, nearly one-third of the British railway station and track network was closed, contributing to the road versus rail debate that still rages today.

Hornby-Dublo was quick to capitalize on the move to diesel, announcing in December 1958 its model of the 1,000hp Type 1 D8000 Bo-Bo that had emerged from the Vulcan Foundry the previous summer. Numbered L30 then 3230, it was an accurate representation of the original and worked well, but lacked the solidity of the older models. Moulding in plastic allowed for far more detail, but the body shells were light and had to be weighted. They also wear less well than the diecast models, often cracking around the retaining screw in the roof. More seriously, it did not work well as a two-rail model and was withdrawn early.

At the opposite end of the power scale, the next diesel-electric model represented the Type 5 English

Electric Deltic. The Deltic was powered by two Napier two-stroke diesels, which produced a distinctive, percussive engine note – as well as clouds of blue smoke. Rolled out for the East Coast Main Line, the Deltics were the first successes of the new breed of locomotives. Hornby-Dublo introduced them in late 1960 in plain green livery, followed in 1961 by an attractive two-tone green, as 2234 "Crepello" in two-rail and 3234 "St Paddy" in three-rail. Appropriately they were named after racehorses – in real life, the experience for drivers was probably similar to riding in a race, as the Deltics rocked alarmingly at high speed. The model is short by comparison with the original, to allow for the radius of toy track, and the lower section of the body is very vulnerable to chipping or side-swiping lineside accessories, so fine examples are much sought after.

Another independently produced locomotive presented in 1958 was a Type 2 1,200hp Co-Bo diesel-electric, jointly manufactured by Metropolitan-Vickers and Beyer-Peacock. Appearances should not prejudice, but it was remarkably ugly, known even to its admirers as "Object" (Metrovick when feeling kinder). Today, the class is best known as Boco in *Thomas the Tank Engine*. The real locomotive had a dreadful reliability record, and the model was not much more successful.

Although it was not not under the same pressure to export as it had been in the 1940s, Hornby-Dublo still took note of overseas markets. The most unusual item was a special adaptation for the Canadian market, probably carried out at the Meccano warehouse in Toronto. Ordinary Bo-Bo diesel-electric locomotives had their armatures and buffer heads removed to make them into dummy power cars to add to long freight consists. Few genuine examples now exist.

The little Hornby-Dublo six-coupled shunter D3302 came out in two-rail form in late 1960 as 2231, with the 3321 three-rail version following six months later. The original locomotive was a direct descendant of a pre-war LMS design; renumbered as Class 08s after 1967,

below: *This is quite a simple set from 1959, but proof that plastic is not necessarily a poor material when produced to a high standard.*

examples can still be seen in freight sidings today, giving a nostalgic hint of past steam days. The model was fitted with a detailed plastic body and the Ringfield motor, but not to great effect. The unit tended to overheat and suffered from poor traction.

The last two Hornby-Dublo models produced were quite different from the rest of the stable. They were both electric, but served diametrically opposed markets. The first represented an SR Electric Multiple Unit, of the type that served the London suburbs; the second was a 25kv E3000 Bo-Bo, for speeding passengers northwards from London to Birmingham and Manchester.

above: A Bassett-Lowke live-steam "Super Enterprise" from 1955 in attractive BR Brunswick Green. It is hard to find these unscorched, usually as a result of overfilling the burner.

Hornby-Dublo triumphed by fitting the Ringfield motor into the cab of a model of the latest British Railways electric stock. The yellow warning panel is bright and the lithographed body sides gleam, but are vulnerable to scratching and rusting at the edges. For reasons of economy, the bogie side frames are made of clip-on plastic, which often vanish, as they do from the Deltics and the E3002.

The E3000 electric locomotives (later Classes 81 to 85) transformed performance on the London–Manchester route, passing the baton to the similar Class 86s that still run on the West Coast line. The Hornby-Dublo model was based on the AEI prototype and numbered E3002. It was reasonably accurate, but development coincided with financial problems, so the plastic body shell is less detailed than it might have been, with clip-on plastic bogie frames. It finally emerged in two-rail form in September 1964, with three-rail conversions available. The E3002 has legendary status with Hornby-Dublo collectors, as it was the last model produced and few were issued; they are very hard to find in clean boxes with intact inserts. Although not as fine as its predecessors, it was a fitting epitaph to the Hornby-Dublo range.

SUPER DETAIL COACHES AND FREIGHT STOCK

If the Ringfield motor was the high point of Hornby-Dublo motor design, then the Super Detail coach was the zenith of passenger stock. As a rough rule of thumb, any coach in the 4000 series is interesting to collectors, being either an improved older model, or one of the completely new range introduced in December 1960.

The new bogie passenger stock combined the best of old and new: lightweight and crisply moulded plastic under-frames, ends and roofs with finely lithographed sides. Through their experience with Dinky Toys, Meccano Ltd had much experience in scaling down from prototype to toy. If done by exact reduction, a toy would look too flimsy and model-like; certain details and proportions had to be exaggerated to make the piece look good from a height, and the length had to be short enough to accommodate track curves. A perfectionist could carp at missing details, but they were intended as durable toys, although at a cost – in the mid-1960s, one could have bought one-and-a-half Corgi Toy James Bond Aston Martin DB5s for the same price.

Much of the stock produced was in BR maroon, representing Western, Midland and Eastern Regions; the sleeping and restaurant cars are particularly popular. A rare oddity was a six-wheel passenger brake or "stove", modelled on a short Clemenson-type coach with lateral movement in the centre axle. Three Pullman coaches, packed with interior detail, looked good, but were so light that they tended to foul on points.

The proof of the success of these coaches was their superb performance on the track – they ran smoothly and, being relatively light, could be hauled in long rakes with ease. The only problem was to fit a long enough station platform on a layout. At the time of closure, huge amounts of stock were left over, and Super Detail stock was still available from certain outlets in the early 1980s.

Hornby-Dublo introduced a novel item in March 1957 that went some way to emulating the busy and entertaining electrical accessories produced by the Americans. The Travelling Post Office Coach had a pivoted metal section at the back that was flicked open by a solenoid operated by an electric lineside contact rail. The forward part then ejected a diecast mail sack into an enclosure, while the rear part snatched a fresh sack from a hook a split second later, all achieved amid much noise and some sparks.

The first Super Detail freight vehicle, a bulk grain wagon introduced in February 1958, differed completely from the dull BR tinplate range. The frame was neatly diecast and the body was moulded plastic, both packed with realistic detail and combining lightness and accuracy with strength. Over the next four years the range

below: *The finest post-war Bassett-Lowke 0 Gauge locomotive in series production was the magnificent and powerful three-rail electric BR "Duchess of Montrose" from 1957.*

extended to include fish vans, hopper wagons, wagons for coal, glass, cement and salt and even a crane set. Sought-after items include the maroon or green horse boxes (with plastic horse), flat wagon with tractor or plastic cable drums and a caustic liquor bogie tank wagon with rare diamond-shaped bogie frames. The rarest of all is a rapidly adapted humble mineral wagon: it was given a coat of black paint, had tubes for two cigarette filters cast into the base and a special "Rail Cleaning Wagon" transfer. It was only issued in tiny numbers after the Lines Bros takeover, so is extremely sought after in boxed condition (see page 148).

TRAIN SETS AND ACCESSORIES

The last years of Hornby-Dublo produced several rare train sets. The P20 "Bristolian" included the "Bristol Castle" locomotive and the G25 included the 8F 2–8-0 (P stood for Passenger and G for Goods). The rarest, in beautiful blue and white boxes with pictorial lids, appeared only from 1962 to 1963: 2033 included the Metrovick Co-Bo; 2034 the Deltic "Crepello"; 2049 was

a breakdown train and 2050 was a Southern Region two-car suburban electric multiple unit. Rarest of all is the 2035 "Bournemouth Belle" set, which consisted of the rebuilt West Country class "Barnstaple" and three Pullmans in a box with vacu-formed plastic liner. This crucial feature means that a set auctioned in 1996 reached a world record price.

The last sets produced by Hornby-Dublo were known as Starter Sets, made as a last-ditch attempt to provide a competitively priced ready-made layout. This was only achieved by slashing the quality of the contents and packing, and the resulting sales were dismal. This makes them scarce and so, despite the poor quality, they are sought after in good condition.

During its reinvestment programme, Meccano was not content just to upgrade existing accessories. It spent large sums of money with British Industrial Plastics Tools Ltd to have the finest possible tooling made, from which flowed an extraordinary range of fine items to decorate the new two-rail layouts, from a large terminal station, goods depot and tunnels to colour light signals, lineside

when it closed and sold the tooling to Dapol. Although production could start again in Llangollen, for the time being the spirit of Hornby-Dublo remains just a happy memory.

FRENCH HORNBY

In the 1940s and 1950s the French factory continued to plough its own furrow, just as it had done before the war. French buyers of Hornby were doubly fortunate: not only did the range continue to expand in interesting ways, but the Bobigny factory carried on producing 20-volt electric locomotives and track, including the streamlined "Etoile du Nord", withdrawn in 1954. In the same year the silver pre-war-based PO electric locomotive was replaced with a tinplate-bodied one of modern appearance. Not long before the 0 Gauge range ceased in 1963–4, two diecast-bodied 20-volt DC electric locomotives were introduced. They were both mounted on a pair of neat four-wheel bogies, one of which was powered. The TZB was a "steeple-cab" type locomotive and the TNB was a Bo-Bo of the type currently achieving record running speeds on SNCF passenger services. Both were far superior to any post-war offerings from Binns Road.

In the same way as 0 Gauge pieces developed independently in France, so in 1959 the Bobigny factory launched an entirely new H0 Gauge range, called AcHO after the phonetic pronunciation of the initials in French.

Hornby-Dublo may have been more solid, but it was left far behind in attention to scale detail, and the French designers achieved extraordinary crispness with the use

above: *The Bassett-Lowke "Flying Scotsman" looks especially fine lithographed in the experimental BR blue of the period from 1949 to 1952.*

notices and passengers and station staff. The garish red plastic girder bridge with two base colours, available only from 1963 to 1964, was a much finer model than its diecast predecessor but is now extremely hard to find.

THE END OF AN ERA

The end of the original Hornby-Dublo and Meccano Ltd was an object lesson in the sad result of building to a standard rather than a price. The habit of superb quality died hard, and the E3002 electric locomotive shows how poor the range would have become if forced to cut corners. As in many ways, where the company led others followed; within twenty-five years most European toy and train manufacturers were bankrupt or producing in the Far East.

Although the company lost its independence, some stock and spares were still in Tri-ang–Hornby price lists until 1966–7, when G&R Wrenn took over part of the stock and tooling. Wrenn's main concern was to build up a new range of high-quality 00 Gauge railways, largely based on Hornby-Dublo tooling. This it did until 1993, of high-quality plastic mouldings. The electric locomotives were all modern types; several are now very collectible. The green suburban coaches are plain and very much in the shadow of the fine "inox" corrugated silver express coaches that rivalled the product of any contemporary maker. The freight was also detailed to the point of being fragile, particularly the stake wagon and the coach wheel-carrying flat truck. The AcHO Station and Signal Cabin may look rather over-stylized by the standards of today, but they were far ahead of the safe styling from Binns Road. Despite the continued success of Hornby AcHO, it was eventually dragged down by the failure of Lines Bros in 1971, and finally closed in 1972.

BASSETT-LOWKE

Wenman Bassett-Lowke and his guests had much to celebrate at a series of fiftieth anniversary dinners in 1949 and 1950. Surrounded by colleagues, businessmen, clients and old friends such as Franz Bing and Siegfried Kahn, Bassett-Lowke could look back on years of success and innovation, and some of the finest toy and model locomotives ever made. Production had already restarted after war work, but the future looked uncertain.

below: Edward Exley went on producing superb LMS passenger stock for many years after nationalization and much was sold through Bassett-Lowke's catalogues.

In 1941 the name of Winteringhams had been changed to Precision Models Ltd, and after the war several of their familiar pre-war locomotives were revived, including the 0–6–0 tank locomotive and the Mogul. The roster of Pacifics included the "Flying Scotsman" and the "Duchess of Montrose" but, sadly, neither of the pre-war streamliners. The "Royal Scot" appeared in rebuilt form in 1948, far outshining its pre-war antecedents in its LMS black livery. In 1953 it reappeared in its final form in BR green livery, with boiler banding and lining and a replica of its special nameplate detailing its trip to America in 1932.

A more typical and affordable product was the elegant LMS 4–6–0 "Super Enterprise" from 1950. The following year the "Duke of York" 4–4–0 was revived as the "Prince Charles", in blue and then green BR livery. It was quite popular, but the workmanship on the later examples is poor, showing what skills had been lost. The "Super Enterprise" never compared in beauty with the BR "Duchess of Montrose" (see pages 166 and 167).

The most successful Bassett-Lowke Pacific was the "Flying Scotsman". The rarest version followed the search in the early days of British Railways for a new livery. From the autumn of 1949 until around 1952, blue was the colour for express passenger locomotives (see page 168);

she was modelled in this state and collectors can expect to pay 50 per cent more than for the regular liveries. Having said this, it still looks smart in the normal BR green livery – and without her current Germanic smoke deflectors.

Curiously, some of the very last locomotives, built in the late 1950s, are among the hardest to find. These include the BR Standard Pacific "Britannia", the 4–6–0 Class V, the Deltic prototype and special models built to order for Bassett-Lowke by the celebrated builder Vic Hunt, such as an extremely elusive BR 2–8–0 8F freight locomotive.

Bassett-Lowke did produce a range of tinplate rolling stock and British Railways coaches in maroon and cream, but sadly they are rather plain and charmless. The company was fortunate in having the services of Edward Exley as a subcontractor, because his firm's work is always a pleasure to look at. LMS stock turns up most often, followed by GWR. The LNER tourist buffets are sought after but, perversely, the BR "plum and spilt milk" coaches are among the rarest of all.

The problems facing Bassett-Lowke can be put into context by looking at two catalogues, from 1953 – the year that Bassett-Lowke himself died – and 1956. In the earlier catalogue can be found only Bassett-Lowke's own products, including the dependable "Duchess of Montrose". By 1956, the same "Duchess" costs 10 per cent more and the catalogue includes 00 Gauge railways from Trix – as would be expected – but also Hornby-Dublo and Tri-ang. With a Hornby-Dublo "Duchess of Montrose" priced at twice as much as a Tri-ang R0 "Princess Elizabeth", the future was not hard to anticipate. Even the cheaper Bassett-Lowke 0 Gauge range could not compete, and Trix was usually a liability, finally being sold in February 1957.

Eventually, in 1964, the shop at 112 High Holborn was sold to Beattie's. The company survived until 1969, when it became Bassett-Lowke Railways Ltd and was involved with Alan Pegler, the pioneer preservationist who saved the "Flying Scotsman" and took it on its inspired but expensive North American tour. The company then went through several changes of ownership, but collectors and enthusiasts never lost sight of its special qualities. The name now belongs to Corgi, which is currently selling well-built live-steam 0 Gauge BR and LMS Moguls. Like most toys today, they are built in China.

above: *The 1948 Lionel 0 Gauge General Motors F3 diesel sets were well designed and sturdy, although the bodies were made of plastic.*

TRIX TWIN AND TRIX EXPRESS

There was tremendous pent-up demand for Trix products between 1946 and 1950. This kept the Precision Models factory in Stimpson Avenue, Northampton, busy to capacity, as well doing contract jobs for Bassett-Lowke. In practice, the survival of the business relied very much on Siegfried Kahn, who worked tirelessly with tiny retained profits, and a loyal workforce. They endured great hardships in primitive conditions with frequent power and fuel shortages.

Trix in Nürnberg was in even worse shape: war damage meant that production did not restart until 1947 and the first post-war catalogue was issued in 1949. In 1950, Franz Bing and his sister eventually gained restitution for the enforced loss of their company under the Nazis and the management of the British and German companies moved together again. They worked on joint projects such as use of the new 12-volt DC motor introduced in Germany in 1954. One unsuccessful introduction was the overpriced "Meteor", an American-style diesel three-car unit launched at the end of 1955. Although it was an exciting and noisy runner, with effective lighting, it was a rather non-specific freelance design and found few takers.

below: *In 1957 Lionel sought to expand its market to include girls by manufacturing this pastel pink locomotive. It was rejected by everyone at the time, but collectors are fond of it now.*

Trix also made some eccentric product choices, such as its costly Mineral Train Set, which came complete with magnetically operated tipping hopper wagons and a huge elevator conveyor that lifted coal or ore and transferred it by rubber belt to the other side of the layout.

One smart move was an association with Michael Catalani, a design genius. In October 1956 he was commissioned to fit the new German 12-volt DC motor into both existing and new locomotives, and he put in hand the finest locomotives produced by Trix, although sadly their production span was short. By February 1957 he had pre-production models ready, and the revised Hunt Class "Pytchley" appeared. For 1958–9, Catalani designed a fine BR Standard Pacific "Britannia" and BR Class V, which would no doubt have been more successful had the company been in better shape. Other interesting models followed: the EM1 "Triton", a Class 66xx ex-GWR tank locomotive and, the last model to be produced with a diecast body, the Bo-Bo diesel "Warship" class. By this

time, British Trix's financial position was rocky. Ewart Holdings had taken over in February 1957, but the company went into receivership the following October, just as new lines were beginning to come through. Only a quarter of the staff were re-hired in November under the new owners, Dufay Ltd, a camera and photographic supplies manufacturer. Production was moved to Birmingham in 1960, but business still did not thrive and Courtaulds took over the company in 1963. Despite the inspired designs of Ernst Rozsa, British Trix found itself up for sale again in 1968.

In the plastic-body British Trix era under Courtaulds, a fine E3001 West Coast electric locomotive was followed by the Western diesels, the Trans-Pennine DMU and a well-detailed model of the "Flying Scotsman". (After 1968 this came with two tenders, following the running practice of the prototype, which had to haul an extra tender to carry water, as British Railways had removed all the lineside water towers.)

German Trix then did a reverse takeover of British Trix, to produce Thernglade Ltd under Rozsa. When the German company merged with GAMA (George Adam Mangold, a famous German toymaker), Rozsa kept various related businesses going into the 1990s in loyal support of a great name.

LIONEL

After 1945, Lionel entered a period of sustained high sales. There were countless additions to the range: milk can loaders, livestock loading pens and helicopter cars were among them. The imposing electric Pennsylvania GG1 was modelled, as well as a turbine loco and a wide range of well-proportioned diesels (see page 171). Once again a small gauge was offered, but it was only a half-hearted effort to sell H0 equipment manufactured cheaply for Lionel.

The end of the boom years came in 1957 and the company went rapidly downhill. After that Lionel began losing money and floundered about for new direction. A hideous pink steam locomotive for girls was one of the failures, although today it is highly collectible. After Cowen sold the company in 1959, the trains were still made but the company fortunes were variable. New owners, such as General Mills and Richard Kughn, came and went. Despite everything, Lionel is still the major US toy train manufacturer. It is an interesting observation that the vast majority of toy train collectors in the US are now interested in Lionel products from 1970 to the present.

BUILDING UP A COLLECTION

It is possible to enjoy toy trains without collecting them, but once the fascination is there, collectors and their families can become surrounded by the paraphernalia of addiction to toy trains. In many collecting hobbies, the chosen object remains static in a display case, but trains have the added dimension of play value. Planning and constructing a running layout can take years and can be as complex and realistic as you wish. There is then the thrill of the chase, hunting out sought-after pieces to run on a layout or to put on display.

Buying at an auction

Auctions are some of the best places to buy when when you are forming a collection. Most auction houses describe the contents of each lot in detail and give an objective assessment of its cosmetic condition as well. They do not usually state mechanical condition, unless there is a glaring fault such as a broken spring or a missing driving wheel.

A good auction, such as Christie's Trains Galore auction, is a social gathering as well as a bidding opportunity. The atmosphere is not at all intimidating and room bidders are put at ease by experienced auctioneers. They will not knock anything down to someone scratching their nose, but they will return to someone who has shown interest. Bidders vary in their tactics – sitting in different places in the room or even moving around.

Lots are on view prior to the auction, but you can also leave absentee bids if you are unable to attend. Sale catalogues are available one month before the auction date, and the sale lots with photographs are also available on many auction houses' websites. In addition to the hammer price there is a buyer's premium to be paid, but the auction process means that a buyer will pay a fair price on the day; only time can tell whether that is a low or a high price.

1 This is a good example of "buyer beware". Here are the remains of a Märklin Gauge I live-steam Pacific, used as the basis for the "Flying Scotsman", the "Lord Nelson" and "The Great Bear" (for a perfect and unused example, see page 74). The difference in quality – and value – between these examples is instructive. Live-steam locomotives have often had a hard life, but this one has had many parts replaced with poorly crafted handmade pieces, including the tender. It has also been stripped of all paint.

Buying privately

The best dealers have enviable contacts that enable them to find top-quality pieces from private sources, avoiding the auction route altogether. However, it is fair to expect to pay a premium price for items sold by people of this calibre; they will be able to give first-class advice with excellent knowledge. Most dealers take tables at the many toy and train fairs that take place across Britain, mainland Europe and the USA every weekend. There, collectors will find a vast amount of material to chose from, usually governed by *caveat emptor* (buyer beware). It is vital to know your subject and to remember that gems can be found on or below any table at any time of day. Be aware that poor lighting in many halls can either obscure or distort paint colours, or conceal restored pieces.

2 Fortunately, the belief that the supply of collectible toy trains and accessories hidden in cellars and attics may be drying up can still be disproved. Apart from the massive Märklin Gauge V train discovered in a barn (see page 55), this little sibling turned up in old suitcases. Selling well above estimate, it is exactly what collectors like to see – a very rare British export Märklin Gauge III LNWR locomotive and tender in original "undiscovered" condition.

Buying for investment

In short, don't. The only income that a true collector can expect is one of pleasure; an increase in value can only be an added bonus. As with equities, valuations vary all the time. Although they are an alternative to cash in inflationary times, toy trains do not generate income unless traded all the time – indeed, insurance and security are expensive. The best rule seems to be to buy the best that you can possibly afford and always aim for pieces in good original condition. It is far better to have a small collection of fine pieces than a huge and unfocused collection of poor-quality items, unless they are to be used for repainting or running. The market is usually overflowing with such toy trains and starved of true rarities.

3 and 4 These two Hornby wagons serve as examples of what to buy and what not to buy. The Brake Van is from the 1950s BR era. It is in poor shape and is all but worthless – unless for repainting practice. The "Colas" Bitumen Wagon, on the other hand, is gleaming and something to aspire to at almost any price.

COLLECTORS' INFORMATION

Introduction: Tinplate – at the heart of toy railways

The invention of sheet steel coated with rust-inhibiting tin provided a material that was indispensable for much of the toy railway industry until the 1950s. Tinplate was light, strong and durable; it could be folded, pressed, punched, soldered, tabbed, painted and lithographed with great success. It could be used for simple pieces made by unskilled labour or for complex masterpieces of soldering crafted by expert tinsmiths.

In around 1900, Bing and Märklin produced toy railways that came as close as possible to artistry, with exquisite craftsmanship, hand painting and lacquering. By 1903, rotary off-set lithography had streamlined the business, particularly in Nürnberg. It enabled the rapid and highly detailed printing of flat tinplate sheet, which was then stamped out and tabbed into a huge variety of locomotives, rolling stock or accessories. A fine British example is the Bassett-Lowke LNER "Flying Scotsman" locomotive.

After 1920, Hornby used lithography extensively and with great success; much of the production was subcontracted to Hudson, Scott and Sons in Carlisle. For paintwork, Hornby used ovens to bake it to a durable and lustrous finish.

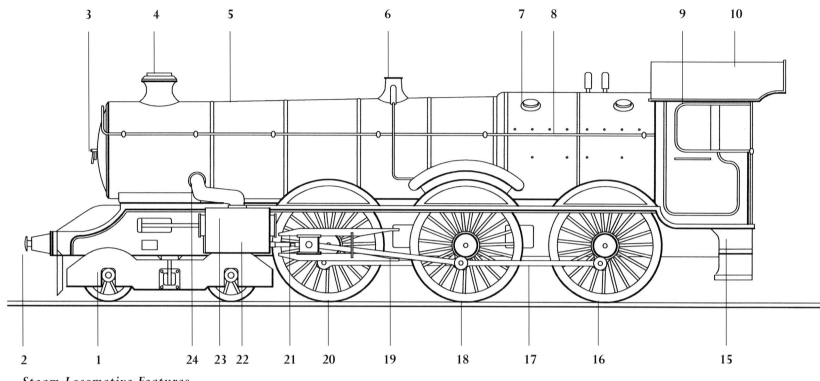

Steam Locomotive Features

Glossary

Backhead The area in the cab at the back of a steam locomotive where the driver's controls are located.

Box car American term for a goods van or freight car.

Bogie A group of four or six wheels in the same frame, supporting each end of a passenger coach or wagon with a central pivot. On diesel or electric locomotives, bogies can be powered ("A" end) or non-powered ("B" end). Occasionally, in order to spread axle loading, large locomotives are built with three bogies; the Anglo-French Channel Tunnel "Shuttle" locomotives are examples. Known as trucks in America.

Caboose American term for a goods brake van.

Car American term for British coach or wagon.

Clerestory Raised centre section of a coach roof with glazed sides, named after the band of windows running along the upper nave of some medieval Gothic cathedrals.

Cowcatcher Pointed metal grid frame on the front of a locomotive for deflecting eponymous creatures or other objects. Sometimes called a "pilot" in America and a "Kuhfängen" in Germany.

Cut-off Steam inlet into both sides of locomotive pistons controlled by valve gear; control of cut-off is crucial to smoothly controlled starting and running.

Double heading Two locomotives hauling a train together. Usually the front one would be a banking engine, kept on hand to help out on long and heavy gradients.

Ducket Guard's glazed lookout protruding from the side of a British brake van. The US and Continental version protruded from the roof.

Fall-plates Hinged metal plate to cover the gap between locomotive and tender or two coaches

Firebox The chamber at the heart of a steam locomotive in which burning coal heated water to create steam. The fireman's job was arduous, as loading coal from the cab was

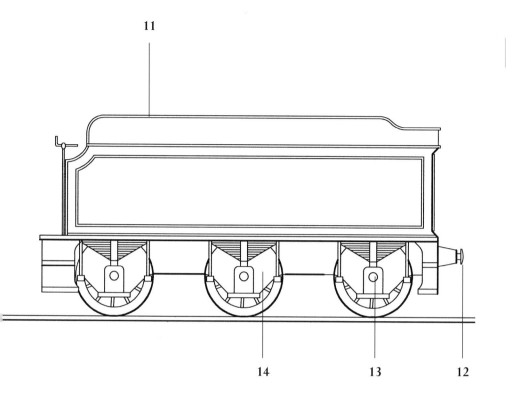

11

14   13   12

Key to Illustration

1	Bogie	13	Axle box
2	Buffer and buffer beam	14	Axle guard
3	Smokebox door	15	Cab step
4	Chimney	16	Trailing wheel
5	Boiler	17	Coupling rod
6	Safety valve	18	Driving wheel
7	Firebox	19	Connecting rod
8	Handrail	20	Leading wheel
9	Backhead (controls)	21	Crosshead
10	Cab	22	Outside cylinder and piston
11	Tender	23	Valves
12	Coupling	24	Main steam pipe to cylinder

tough work and the correct water levels and air intake had to be maintained at all times.

Gondola American term for an open wagon.

Goods brake van British term for a caboose.

Goods van British term for a box car.

Open wagon British term for a gondola.

Permanent way Overall term for track, sleepers and ballast.

Pilot American term for cowcatcher.

Pony British term for two-wheeled truck on a locomotive.

Power Ratings, UK A unified system was introduced under British Railways to cope with the many locomotives inherited from different companies. Locomotives were graded by power from 1 to 8 and lettered P for passenger or MT for Mixed Traffic – 5MT, for example. Freight locomotives were graded on a different power rating from 1 to 9 and lettered F – 9F, for example.

Rake The arrangement of coaching or freight stock behind a locomotive.

Running boards Long steps running along coaches and wagons just above axle-box level.

Smokebox Area at the front of a locomotive operating at working pressure, where steam passing through the boiler tubes and the exhaust and ash from the firebox meet below the chimney. A circular door with sturdy bolts gives access to allow cleaning and maintenance.

Tank locomotive British term for a locomotive running without a tender, so storing water in tanks around the boiler and coal in a bunker behind the cab. Confusingly known as a "Tenderlokomotive" in Germany.

Truck American term for a bogie, comprising four or six wheels in a frame under locomotive or rolling stock

Valve gear Complex linkage for controlling the cut-off of the piston stroke on steam locomotives; best known designs include Walschaerts, Heusinger, Caprotti and poppet.

Gauges

With toy trains, the gauge is the distance between rail centres in smaller gauges and inner-rail edge to edge in large gauges. The gauge measurement is the key to the proportional reduction in scale of the toy compared to the full-size locomotive, but different companies modelled rolling stock bodies to differing scales even in the same gauges. Hornby-Dublo is always 00 Gauge, and the scale is 4mm:1ft. H0 gauge is the same track width as 00 Gauge (16.5mm), but the scale is 3.5mm:1ft. Märklin was 00 Gauge until 1948, then H0 Gauge. Tri-ang is 00 Gauge.

TOY TRAIN GAUGES

All makers	OO/H0 Gauge	$^1/_2$in (16.5mm)
All makers	0 Gauge	1in (35mm)
All makers	Gauge I	1in (48mm)
All makers	Gauge II	2in (54mm)
Bassett-Lowke		
Bing Carette	Gauge III	2in (67mm)
Märklin	Gauge III	3in (75mm)
Schönner	Gauge III	3in (75mm)
Bassett-Lowke	Gauge IV	3in (75mm)
Bing	Gauge IV	3in (75mm)

Locomotive wheel arrangements

In Britain and America, locomotive wheel arrangements are designated by a system that enumerates the number of wheels, known as the Whyte notation, introduced in America in around 1900. The naming system is also of American origin, but was widely adopted in Britain. Railwaymen also had their own nicknames for locomotives or classes – not always flattering. The German alphanumeric system is more sophisticated, as the letters denote coupled wheels. The figures denote the number of axles, not wheels.

STEAM LOCOMOTIVES

GB/USA	Name	Germany, Austria and Switzerland
0–4–0		B
0–4–2		B' 1
0–6–0		C
4–4–2	Atlantic	2' B 1'
4–6–4	Baltic (GB)	2' C 2'
4–6–4	Hudson (USA)	
2–8–2	Mikado	
2–6–0	Mogul	1' C
4–8–2	Mountain	2' D 1'
4–6–2	Pacific	2' C 1'
2–6–2	Prairie	1' C 1'

Elsewhere in Europe steam locomotives are enumerated by the axles rather than by the wheels, so the British and American numbers are halved (i.e. 4–6–2 becomes 2–3–1).

DIESEL AND ELECTRIC LOCOMOTIVES

In the USA, the same notation is used as for steam locomotives. In Britain and Europe, a four-wheeled uncoupled powered bogie is designated a "Bo" and a six-wheeled bogie a "Co".

	Name	British examples
Four/four	Bo-Bo	BR Class 20
Six/four	Co-Bo	Metro-Vick
Six/six	Co-Co	Class 47
Four/four/four	Tri-Bo	Channel "Shuttle"

Some railway companies

Great Britain
Pre-grouping (1 January 1923)

CR	Caledonian Railway
GCR	Great Central Railway
GER	Great Eastern Railway
GNR	Great Northern Railway
GWR	Great Western Railway
LB&SCR	London Brighton and South Coast Railway
LNWR	London North Western Railway
LSWR	London and South Western Railway
MR	Midland Railway
NBR	North British Railway
SECR	South East and Chatham Railway

Post grouping

GWR	Great Western Railway
LMS	London Midland and Scottish
LNER	London North Eastern Railway
SR	Southern Railway
BR	British Railways, nationalized railway formed in 1948

Germany

DB	Deutsche Bundesbahn
DR	Deutsche Reichsbahn – grouped 1920, created 1924

France

PLM	Paris–Lyon-Mediterranée
PO	Paris–Orléans
Etat	
Nord	
Midi	
Est	

SNCF	Société Nationale des Chemins de Fer Français, nationalized railway, formed in 1938

Switzerland

SBB/CFF	Schweizerischebundes Bahn/Chemins de Fer Federaux Suisses
BLS	Bern-Lötschberg-Simplon

USA

NYC	New York Central
Santa Fe	
PRR	Pennsylvania Railroad
SP	Southern Pacific
UP	Union Pacific
CNW	Chicago and North Western Railroad
L&N	Louisville and Nashville

Passenger and freight stock notation

In Britain, the wheels are counted; in Germany the axles are counted. Thus, a typical wagon would be described as either four wheel or two axle.

A typical large passenger coach would have two four wheel bogies, which would be four axle in German notation. Very occasionally, passenger vehicles had two six-wheel bogies, such as the LNWR 12-wheeled Dining Car, which would be six-axle in German notation.

Boxes and packaging

Having an original box in good condition is always an asset for a toy train, but it is more important with some makes than others.

Hornby 0 Gauge

For most serious collectors of pre-war Hornby, original boxes are a necessity. The first individual boxes for locomotives and stock were made from plain card. Later boxes were printed in an attractive shiny red, with illustrated ends, later replaced with matt boxes with text on the ends. McCaw, Stevenson and Orr Ltd of Belfast printed most of the packaging for Meccano Ltd (see *The Hornby Railway Collector*, April 2000).

Boxes for small items are still easy to find in good condition, but boxes for the larger locomotives and buildings are not, so fine ones can double the value of the piece. Larger boxes tend to suffer badly from edge splitting and warping. Post-war boxes in good condition are plentiful, little affecting the relatively low value of the contents.

Hornby-Dublo

The long, thin boxes of pre-war sets are fairly uncommon, but are often in poor condition. The light powder-blue boxes for locomotives are very scarce, as are boxes for wooden buildings, and good stock and accessory boxes are not common.

Post-war Goods and Passenger Set boxes were squarer and deeper than the pre-war type, with increased space for presentation of the contents. Some of the earliest examples are much sought after by collectors.

Early post-war Hornby-Dublo boxes came in various styles and shades of blue, always with a helpful date code. Although made from quite sturdy card, the edges tend to go furry very easily, thus losing their fresh appearance.

Beware of misleading railway company labels; these have often been replaced or swapped around.

The earliest Super Detail boxes featured line drawings of the contents on a blue background, with white stripes and descriptive end labels. When the 4000 series was introduced in 1959, the background was changed to red and the images were dropped. The complex multi-purpose flap arrangement of the earlier coach and wagon boxes was replaced by a simpler flap and two tabs, the couplings protected by cheaper card rings.

In the last years of production, boxes for train sets became shallow and broad. They were also very fragile; as a result some collectors shun sets in principle. The boxes for the last locomotives were as smart as the contents: a picture on the lid, with striped background and sides – red for two-rail and blue for three-rail.

Märklin

Early trains are so rare that collectors are not so concerned with the boxes, although they sometimes survive with a paper label giving the correct catalogue reference number for the contents. Sets were sold in more attractive red boxes with illustrated labels.

Most 00 and H0 Gauge collectors see boxes as an absolute necessity. Those for 00 Gauge from 1935 and H0 Gauge from 1948 were plain brown until 1957, when colourful illustrated boxes were introduced.

Restoration and replicas

Restoration is both tricky and expensive. If possible, it should be done using reversible glues and other removable papers and paints.

Reproduction boxes are convenient for collectors but do not generally add value to the contents. Most good makes are clearly identified as replicas, but some are not, and in the wrong hands can be allowed to deceive the unwary buyer.

Bibliography

Several reproduction catalogues and fine books about toy railways are hard to find and are rarities in themselves. Mention of titles in this bibliography does not imply that they can be easily obtained.

Baecker, Carlernst, Haas, Dieter and Jeanmaire, Claude, *Märklin – Technical Toys in the Course of Time*, reprinted original catalogues 1859–1978, Volumes 1 to 15 (Hobby Haas/Verlag Eisenbahn, Villigen, Switzerland, 1975–1992)

Baecker, Carlernst, Haas, Dieter, Jeanmaire, Claude, and Väterlein, Christian, *Die Anderen Nürnberger* (Hobby Haas, Frankfurt am Main, 1973–1988)

Bassett-Lowke & Co., *Catalogue, 1904–1905*, reprint (Token Publishing, Hindhead)

Bassett-Lowke Railways Limited 1968 Catalogue

Carlson, Pierce, *Toy Trains – A History* (Victor Gollancz, London, 1986)

Carpenter, Jeff, *Bing's Table Railway* (Diva Publishing, Sawbridgeworth, 1996)

Ellis, Alan F., *Hornby-Dublo Compendium* (New Cavendish Books, London, 1980)

Foster, Michael, *Hornby-Dublo Trains* (New Cavendish Books, London, 1980)

Frei, Alfred, *Märklin Spur I–IV* (Alfred Frei, Adetswil, 2000)

Frei, Alfred, *Märklin Spur 0* (Alfred Frei, Adetswil, 2000)

Fuller, Roland, *The Bassett-Lowke Story* (New Cavendish Books, London, 1984)

Höllerer, Dr. Ing. O, *Märklin-Handbuch für Ausstattungsstücke zu den großen Spurweiten 1895–1939* (Verlag Dr. O. Höllerer, Munich, 1999)

Koll, Joachim, *Koll's Preis-Katalog Märklin HO/OO 2002* (Verlag Joachim Koll, Bad Homburg v.d.H, 2001)

Levy, Allen, *A Century of Model Trains* (New Cavendish Books, London, 1974)

Levy, Allen, *The Great Toys of Georges Carette – 1911 Trade Catalogue* (New Cavendish Books, London, 1974)

Marsh, Hugo (Consultant), *Toys and Games* (Miller's, London, 2nd edition, 2001)

Matthewman, Tony, *The History of Trix HO/OO Model Railways in Britain* (New Cavendish Books, London, 1994)

Parry-Crooke, Charlotte, *Märklin 1895–1914* (Denys Ingram Publishers, London, 1983)

Schiffmann, Reinhard, *Sammlerkatalog*, (Verlag Reinhard Schiffmann, Volumes 1–11, Forcheim, 1992–2001)

Treichler, Hans Peter, *The Swiss Railway Saga* (AS Verlag & Buchkonzept AG, Zurich, 1996)

Väterlein, Christian, *Biberacher Blechspeilzeug: Masterbook of Rock and Graner, 1875* (Betellius Verlag, Stuttgart, 1997)

Various articles including:

Austin, Albyn, 'A Meccano Mystery Solved – Meccano's Boxmakers' (*The Hornby Railway Collector*, April 2000, p. 9)

Gamble, Jim, 'Raylo', (*The Hornby Railway Collector,* Oct 2000, pp. 8–9)

Hammond, Pat, 'Classic British Railway Modelling' (*British Model Railway Price Guide*, May 2001, p. 4)

Layne, Ian, 'Hudson Scott & Sons: Tinprinters to Hornby' (*The Hornby Railway Collector*: 12 articles Sept 1999–Jan/Feb 2001; detailed and meticulous research into tinprinting for Hornby, with lists of annual production quotas)

Schneider, Lew, 'Hornby's USA-made Trains' (*Classic Toy Trains*, May 2000)

The World Wide Web is also a useful source for esoteric background information.

Christie's addresses

AMSTERDAM

1071 JG Amsterdam
Tel: 31 (0) 20 57 55 255

EDINBURGH

5 Wemyss Place
Edinburgh EH3 6DH
Tel: 44 (0) 131 225 4756

GENEVA

8 Place de la Taconnerie
1204 Geneva
Tel: 41 (0) 22 319 17 66

HONG KONG

2203-5 Alexandra House
16-20 Chater Road
Hong Kong Central
Tel: 852 2521 5396

LONDON

8 King Street
St James's
London SW1Y 6QT
Tel: 44 (0) 20 7839 9060

LONDON

85 Old Brompton Road
London SW7 3LD
Tel: 44 (0) 20 7581 7611

LOS ANGELES

360 North Camden Drive
Beverly Hills CA 90210
Tel: 1 310 385 2600

MELBOURNE

1 Darling Street
South Yarra, Melbourne
Victoria 3141
Tel: 61 (0) 3 9820 4311

MILAN

1 Piazza Santa Maria delle Grazie
20123 Milan
Tel: 39 02 467 0141

MONACO

Park Palace
98000 Monte Carlo
Tel: 377 97 97 11 00

NEW YORK

20 Rockefeller Plaza
New York NY 10020
Tel: 1 212 636 2000

ROME

Palazzo Massimo Lancellotti
Piazza Navona 114
00186 Rome
Tel: 39 06 686 3333

SINGAPORE

Unit 3, Parklane
Goodwood Park Hotel
22 Scotts Road
Singapore 228221
Tel: 65 235 3828

TAIPEI

13F, Suite 302, No. 207
Tun Hua South Road
Section 2
Taipei 106
Tel: 886 2 2736 3356

TEL AVIV

4 Weizmann Street
Tel Aviv 64239
Tel: 972 (0) 3 695 0695

ZURICH

Steinwiesplatz
8032 Zurich
Tel: 41 (0) 1 268 1010

Museum and collectors' club addresses

MUSEUMS

BRIGHTON TOY AND MODEL MUSEUM

52–55 Trafalgar Street
Brighton BN1 4EB
Great Britain

MÄRKLIN MUSEUM

Holzheimer Straße 8
D-73037 Göppingen
Germany

TECHNORAMA

Technoramastraße 2
Wintherthur 8404
Switzerland

THE NATIONAL TOY TRAIN MUSEUM

300 Paradise Lane
Strasburg, PA 17579
USA

COLLECTORS' CLUBS

HRCA (HORNBY RAILWAY COLLECTORS' ASSOCIATION)

PO Box 50
Banbury
Oxon OX15 OXT
Great Britain

BASSETT-LOWKE SOCIETY

George Lane
Stanton
Nr Bury St Edmunds
Suffolk IP31 2UB
Great Britain

THE TRIX TWIN RAILWAY COLLECTORS ASSOCIATION (TTRCA)

36 Sixth Cross Street
Twickenham TW2 5PB
Great Britain

TRAIN COLLECTORS SOCIETY (TCS)

PO Box 20340
London
NW11 6ZE
Great Britain

TRAIN COLLECTORS ASSOCIATION (TCA)

PO Box 248
300 Paradise Lane
Strasburg PA 17579
USA

index

Dedication

To my wife and family and to Chris Littledale, who has forgotten more than I will ever know about toy trains.

HM

To my wife, Eleanor, without whom nothing is possible.

PC

Acknowledgements

HM
Chris Littledale
Pierce Carlson
Nigel Mynheer
Daniel Agnew
Ernie Franklin
Mike and Sue Richardson
Tony Manthos
Gerry Lipkin
Jim Gamble
Lew Schneider
Nicholas Oddy
Pat Hammond
John Ramsay
Paul Barthaud
Jeremy Collins
Tom Rose
Clair Boluski
Nora Amin
Rosie Sharp
Alex McCrindell
Norman Joplin
Mike Ennis
Dr Roger Poulet

Paul Aziz
Anthony Bianco
Mike Foster
David O'Brien
David Pressland
Andrew Hilton
Dagmar Bauer, Gebrüder
Märklin & Cie, GmbH
Joachim Koll
Roberto Julio Milou
And many other friends and
colleagues too numerous to
mention

PHOTOGRAPHERS:
Andy Johnson
Deborah Strutt
Max Saber
Julie Wright
Jimmy Nicola
Cassandre Lavoix
Hugo Marsh

LAYOUT OF GROUP SHOTS:
Hugo Marsh
Chris Littledale

PHOTOGRAPH CREDITS:
All Christie's South Kensington,
except for:
Pierce Carlson (pages 17 (top
and bottom), 32, 33, 40, 42, 49,
53, 58 (bottom), 59 (bottom),
65 (bottom) and 77.)
Chris Littledale (pages 61, 98,
102 (top), 104, 105, 106, 108
(top) and 121.)
Gerry Lipkin (pages 45, 46
(bottom), 50, 51, 52 (top and
bottom), 54 and 64.)
Jim Gamble (page 118)
Gebrüder Märklin & Cie, GmbH
(page 79)
Private Collection (pages 10, 11,
15, 18, 19, 22, 23, 24, 57 and
172).